*I*n addition to beauty, the other thin[g] offers our frontierless age is solace. [A] place where we can reconnect with nature, with our own wildness; with the revering gaze of yesterday's explorers, and with our country's prodigious past. The river gives the soul a place to breathe. It is a place for imaginations to expand. A place where nature still reigns supreme, with horizons undisturbed by structures and banks unencumbered by our suburban endurance race of materialism.

— the author, Brett Dufur, from page 28

Praise for Brett Dufur's Complete Katy Trail Guidebook

"Of all the regional travel guides to the Lewis and Clark Trail, *The Complete Katy Trail Guidebook* is the best. Brett has a lifetime of insider's knowledge of and love for Missouri, and his book will help you find plenty of adventure along the explorers' route."

*— Julie Fanselow, **Traveling the Lewis and Clark Trail***

"I've ridden many of the rails-to-trails projects across the country and often had to scrounge for information. Brett's guidebook is priceless. It's the best rails-to-trails guide I've seen in the United States."

— Thru-biker Hugh Welch, Gatlinburg, Tennessee

"Dufur seems to have picked up a few pointers from William Least Heat Moon, whose *Blue Highways* and *PrairyErth* achieve depth through historical anecdotes and colorful character descriptions... For day-trippers as well as long-distance bikers and hikers, the *Katy Trail Guidebook* is a worthwhile investment. They will do well to make room for it in an easily accessible pocket."

*— Christopher Ryan, **Ozark Sierran***

"Where most guidebook authors finish, Dufur is just getting warmed up... This book contains fun facts not even a history teacher would know."

*— Chuck MacDonald, **St. Louis Times***

"The *Katy Trail Guidebook* is a 'must have' for anyone interested in our Missouri heritage. The book is more than a guidebook for bicyclists and walkers... it is also an insightful look at the history of the Katy Railroad and the many small communities that grew up along the railroad."

*— Franklin McMillan, **Antioch Publication***

Other Books in the Show Me Missouri Series

Exploring Lewis & Clark's Missouri

By Brett Dufur

Illustrations by Kerry Mulvania

When you put your hand in a flowing stream,
you touch the last that has gone before
and the first of what is still to come.
— Leonardo da Vinci

Project support by Martin Bellmann, Nick Bezzerides, James Denny, Everett Dufur, Tawnee Dufur, Walt Goodman, Claire Griffis, Megan Hall, Pippa Letsky, Lesli McClintic, Rob Nix, Cynthia Thompson & Ellen Vaught.

Maps furnished by the U.S. Army Corps of Engineers, Kansas City District.

ISBN 1-891708-15-5   16.95

Pebble Publishing, Inc. • P.O. Box 2 • Rocheport, MO 65279
Phone: (573) 698-3903 • Fax: (573) 698-3108
E-mail: info@pebblepublishing.com
Online: www.pebblepublishing.com

Visit our bookstore in historic Rocheport, Missouri.

To Tawnee & Everett.

To Captain Glen Bishop, who raised an early sail.

To my parents, who have always supported my explorations.

And to the last full-blooded Missouri Indian,
who closed his eyes on this world in 1907.

Acknowledgments

To my many teachers, I thank you all. My formative years of Lewis & Clark exposure occurred on several extended journeys up and down the Missouri River aboard reenactments with the Discovery Expedition of St. Charles. I was like a dry sponge, soaking up Lewis & Clark trivia and banter by leading historians, geographers, educators and hermit river rats that could talk circles around them all. Being aboard those boats allowed me uninterrupted, extended exposure to many of today's noted historians who have helped reconnect today's drylanders with that rolling river teeming with history.

Special thanks go to Gary Moulton for his definitive work on Lewis & Clark published by the Univerity of Nebraska. Thank you for making the unabridged journals so accessible. Without your lifetime of research and published works, many neophyte historians such as myself would simply be up a creek without a paddle.

I would also like to thank Jim Denny for sharing his contagious enthusiasm and for his ability to bring history to life. As the state historian for the Missouri Department of Natural Resources, and as a true river rat passionate about sharing the immense history of his playground, Jim has done more singlehandedly to rekindle the story of Lewis & Clark in Missouri than anyone out there. Jim's research for the Lewis & Clark Expedition Interpretative Sign Project provided some excellent early direction for this book. Look for his book *Atlas of Lewis and Clark in Missouri,* co-authored with James Harlan, published by the University of Missouri Press.

I'd also like to thank the Lewis & Clark community, which has become a second family for me over the past decade: Glen & Joanne Bishop, Mimi & Darold Jackson, Jim & Sue Denny, Crosby Brown, Jim Karpowicz, Bob & Judy Plummer, Peter Geery, Jim & Lou Rascher, Steve Powell, Dave Hibbler, Dave Cain, Gordon Julich, Julie Fanselow, Marcy George, Marci Bennett, Cheryl Thorp, Carol Rudi, Renee Graham, Lorah Steiner, Gary & Sandy Lucy, Matt Nowack, Carolyn Gilman, Scott Mandrell, Blair Chacoine, Don & Jake Taylor, Rod Power, Ken & Linda Green, Porter Williams, C.J. Lanahan, Wayne Crane, Mark Slate, Kevin Kipp, Julie Fanselow, John Becker, Robert Culbertson, Ben Klopfer, Mike & Mary Duncan, Turtle, Corky, "Big Jim" Boyer, "Ole" Olsen, Harry Winland, Jimmy Felder, Dean Clawson, Ruth Colter-Frick, Deb Bailey, Lisa Higgins, Steve Johnson, Bob Dyer, Steve Burdic, Dr. Raymond Wood, Michael Haynes, and all of the crew members of the expeditions I've taken part in. To those who so graciously extended a warm welcome to our crew, I thank you all for some of the best memories of our lives.

A special thanks to the team at *Missouri Life Magazine*: Danita Allen Wood, Greg Wood, Sona Pai, Lin Teasley, Amy Stapleton, Drew Barton and Colleen Mahon. It has been a pleasure working with you all on the seven-part Lewis & Clark series we collaborated on this year. Having that series published as *Lewis & Clark's Journey Across Missouri*—a full-color, coffee-table book—is a dream come true for me.

I'd also like to thank the hundreds of volunteers who donate untold hours to bring the story to life for today's explorers. And special thanks to geographer Kim Penner and the helpful staff at the U.S. Army Corps of Engineers, Kansas City District, for providing the excellent maps used in this book.

To my wife, Tawnee, and son, Everett, I'd like to say thank you for joining me on our own voyage of discovery... As Mark Twain once said, "Sometimes it's better to travel than to arrive."

Table of Contents

Page references to specific communities and specific journal entry dates can be found in the index, which starts on page 251.

Return Downriver to St. Louis:
Ready to Be Home At Last

End Matter

Letter from Rocheport
Missouri River Mile Marker 186.4

Writing this guidebook has been a very rewarding experience. I've always been lured by the rivers and the rolling hills of river country. I have always been drawn to explore those great end-of-the-road towns and to meet the interesting people I always find there.

For the past ten years, I've been living and breathing Lewis & Clark—doing reenactments on the keelboat and pirogues of the Discovery Expedition of St. Charles, introducing friends to the bliss of paddling that quiet river under a full moon, hiking conservation areas, endlessly riding and writing about the Katy Trail in my *Complete Katy Trail Guidebook,* churning out Lewis & Clark websites, doing slide shows and publishing photographs of my river adventures.

In addition to my personal wanderings and explorations, for several years I have coordinated and led press tours for the Missouri Division of Tourism, guiding journalists from other states who wanted to come here and see the Lewis & Clark Trail firsthand. I've trekked and traipsed the Lewis & Clark Trail in Missouri numerous times, with curious journalists in tow, showing them all the highlights of our state. They always left dripping with story ideas—total saturation.

We take for granted how much history is under each step we take in this state, but along the river, we're literally swimming in history. I have met a lot of travelers on Lewis and Clark bus tours that skim the Missouri portion in one day: St. Charles in the morning, Rocheport or Arrow Rock for lunch, then they try to reach Fort Osage near Kansas City just before the fort's visitor center closes. I pity those folks.

My great hope with this guidebook is that travelers in Lewis & Clark's footsteps will slow down and really enjoy today's trail. I think the Lewis & Clark Trail in Missouri is Missouri's premiere outdoor and history playground. The "trail," to me, encompasses the Missouri River, the Katy Trail, the towering bluffs and a treasure-trove of public lands that dot the river banks from the southeast corner of the Mississippi all the way across the state to the northwestern tip past St. Joe. Many other states lack such a connection with their past.

Living in Rocheport, Missouri, I've met many Lewis & Clark trekkies doing the whole trail. They often find that to really explore Lewis & Clark's Missouri, you have to get off the highway. More important than this guidebook is your willingness to open yourself up for a voyage all your own. You are traveling through rural Missouri, where people will often bend over backwards to help you out. Oftentimes, they have a few minutes to tell you about a particular area, stop or give you some directions to other area highlights.

As important as your gas card on this trip is your ability to say "Hi," "Hello," and "How are you!" to the locals. Don't have such a rigid plan that you fail to soak in the local flavor of the interesting people in the many little towns that dot the whole trail in Missouri. There are hundreds of unforgettable river hamlets dotting the river's edge—that's the real treasure of the trip. They are what continues to lure me to the end of the road— right where you have to turn left or right or you end up in the drink. Get off the highways and stay off! You have to be willing to take a chance to explore some dusty road meandering down towards the river. You have to be willing to chuck the highway/ fast food mentality and go native. Eat at diners surrounded by muddy pickup trucks, ask questions of locals, visit county museums and find out where the best riverviews are. Ask directions. And be willing to get completely lost.

Exploring the Lewis & Clark story in Missouri is a lot of fun. Unlike some portions of the trail out west that are in the middle of nowhere (that is, away from modern-day conveniences), the Lewis and Clark Trail in Missouri is relatively easy to explore—giving you the solitude and that elusive "back of beyond" feeling in the beautiful rolling river hills without having to leave the comforts we've all come to expect—I mean this is supposed to be a vacation after all!

What's so interesting about the bicentennial is that no two people are going to experience it the same. The trail rewards both the weekenders visiting the many wonderful community events scheduled across the state, and the trail also rewards those that immerse themselves even deeper. No matter how you explore the trail: by car, by bike or by keelboat, you'll end up with some wonderful outings, adventures and memories.

In this guidebook, you'll quickly find that some tiny towns have more coverage than the bigger trail stops. Many of my fondest travel memories involve the out-of-the-way places we almost missed. This guidebook gives me the chance to highlight those places that might get overlooked amidst all the hoopla. That's why little hamlets like Huntsdale and Bonnot's Mill have bigger entries than St. Louis.

You might also wonder how I chose the featured artists in this book. Highlighting all of the artists along the trail could be a book of its own. I only highlighted a handful of the artists that have studios open to the public along the trail. There are many, many more excellent painters, potters and other artists out there that continue to use the river for their inspiration and their muse. Ask about them when you travel the trail.

And last but not least, I ask a special favor of you, the reader. Please do me a favor at some point and put this book down and seek out the local historians who know this trail like the back of their hand. They will surely direct you to additional unforgettable river hamlets, scenic treasures and gorgeous riverviews.

Perhaps if Lewis & Clark were to travel the trail today, in addition to the overwhelming number of references to "butifull," and "mosquitors" would be an equally misspelled nod to the fine inhabitants of the trail today. Whatever you need, I'm sure you'll find a helping hand not very far away.

Brett

*We were now about to penetrate a country at
least two thousand miles in width, on which the
foot of civilized man had never trodden; the
good or evil it had in store for us was
for experiment yet to determine.*
— Meriwether Lewis

Introduction

The Lewis & Clark Expedition seems to capture the imagination of many readers, whether it be a retired military vet impressed with the Captain's composure in the face of relentless struggles, or a young girl enamored with the story of Sacagawea and her young son, Jean Baptiste. The expedition gives many of us a way to connect with their personal story of triumph over arduous challenges.

Who could have imagined that a $2,500 investment—the amount initially appropriated by Congress to fund the expedition—would continue to create such dividends for historians even 200 years later? In an historical sense, the country has been made richer by this epic story of exploration. It offers a direct connection to a pivotal moment in our country's past, it offers a firsthand glimpse into the natural world the explorers discovered, it puts us face to face with Native American tribes across the country and lures us with its romanticized tales of adventure. Indeed, that ingrained desire to explore and that never-ending westward draw have become as much a part of the American fabric as baseball and apple pie.

This guidebook will focus on subjects sure to interest any Lewis and Clark aficionado. It will highlight William Clark's journal entries as they journeyed across Missouri, with suggestions for places to go and things to do as you and your family head out to rediscover Lewis & Clark's Missouri. And there is much to see and do! In addition, we'll explore what happened to the crew after the expedition returned, and more.

For a complete listing of Lewis & Clark related events, visit www.visitmo.com. For a complete listing of the Discovery Expedition of St. Charles' reenactment schedule, visit lewisandclark.net.

The Corps of Discovery spent 66 days in the present-day state of Missouri, where they rarely made more than 12 miles of progress a day. They advanced 195 miles up the Mississippi River in 1803 traveling to their winter camp at Wood River,

Cottonwood trees shade the river's edge as a red pirogue paddles up slower moving waters outside of the Missouri River's main current.

Illinois. They then traversed nearly 600 additional miles across the state by way of the Missouri River in 1804, enduring relentless "mosquitors & ticks," oftentimes coating their exposed skin in bear fat to elude the onslaught.

To Missouri's great fortune, Lewis and Clark started measuring their course and distance at the mouth of the Ohio River. This allows us to re-create with James Harlan's meticulously researched maps the progress of Lewis & Clark. According to Harlan, there were 70 outward-bound (1803 – 1804) campsites adjacent to or within the present state of Missouri, and 51 of these sites were calculated to fall within the present boundaries of Missouri, with nine in Illinois, seven in Kansas and three in Nebraska. Look for his book *Atlas of Lewis and Clark in Missouri,* co-authored with James Denny, published by the University of Missouri Press. It is available from Pebble Publishing, Inc. by calling (573) 698-3903.

For the next two and a half years, they were to travel close to 8,000 miles through terra incognita, traveling to the headwaters of the Missouri, crossing the Rocky Mountains and following the Clearwater, Snake and Columbia Rivers to the Pacific Ocean and back again. On their return home to St. Louis, the expedition spent another 14 days within the state of Missouri in September of 1806.

After a triumphant arrival at the St. Charles and St. Louis Riverfronts, many members of the Corps of Discovery, including the two captains, made Missouri their home. And so we will explore what happened to the crew and the lasting contributions they made to our state long after their last mile of river was paddled.

Enjoy reading about the Voyage of Discovery that began and ended in Missouri, literally in our own backyard. May this guidebook offer you and your family opportunities to rediscover Missouri and the wonders still to be found there.

The River Revisited:

Reflections in the Wake

of Lewis & Clark

The Original Superhighway—the Missouri River

*I*n 1804, the land we now know as Missouri was incalculably inaccessible to travel. The Missouri River flowed like a brushstroke of good fortune and fate for the indigenous peoples and wildlife to be found there. That place was the Pekitanoui, or River of the Big Canoes. The river and land were connected. The river brought life. Rivers created habitat by flooding the lands seasonally, which created a biologically rich stew that supported a multitude of flora and fauna. Imagine a river valley teeming with life, with buffalo, black bear, elk and deer. It was a veritable Garden of Eden.

For the explorers and the generations of pioneers to follow, that river was to become the United States' original superhighway: the Missouri River. It was a portal so important to the 19th century that transportation, commerce and communication were to be changed forever.

But for many people today, rivers are good for only so many things, like making a painting beautiful, or serving as a wonderful foreground to frame a setting sun. In essence, rivers are scenic, but most people can essentially take them or leave them.

Today, it's impossible to put ourselves in the proper state of mind to imagine a scene from the year 1804. Despite the fact that the river valley had been inhabited by Native Americans for centuries, and had been explored by the French Canadians for the better part of a century, Lewis & Clark were largely entering terra incognita. Perhaps today we just know too much to be able to appreciate the palpable mysteries that reached beyond the explorer's gaze. Theirs was a world of unknown lands—where lifetimes of discoveries awaited.

From Flintlocks to Stealth Bombers in 200 Years

Today, exploration of the unknown has largely been replaced with information saturation. We live in an age obsessed with information. We are swimming in the deep end of a pool full of knowledge. Any random search on the Internet for "Missouri River" or "Rocky Mountains" brings up a quarter of a million entries. We seem to have explored and measured all things, from the world's tallest mountain to the deepest blackness of the ocean.

In 200 years, we have also seen technology progress from the Corps' single shot flintlock to today's Stealth bombers. A cell phone can instantly put us in touch with anyone, anywhere. Television programs of even questionable merit instantly broadcast to more than 70 countries.

Whereas the notes that became the original Lewis & Clark journals were not published for eight years, visitors to modern-day reenactments on replicas of Lewis & Clark's keelboat expect daily photographs and journal updates on the crew's website (http://lewisandclark.net).

And so it is literally impossible for our minds to fathom the realities of Lewis & Clark's world. One historian wrote that then-president Thomas Jefferson lived in a 3-mile-an-hour world, where information traveled by horseback and no faster.

Theirs was a world where some maps were like pages out of a coloring book—largely blank sheets with defined edges, with lots of white space in the middle. Our continent east of the Mississippi River was already colored in. But heading west of the Mississippi River, that map was waiting for William Clark to fill it in.

Explorers Skirting the Edge of Myth & Reality

It's not as if Lewis & Clark were the first to travel up the Missouri River. So why all the excitement? Well, history creates its own heroes. And what Lewis & Clark did was take a trip unlike anything we had seen before, or since. The Corps of Discovery is considered by many as one of the most successful military expeditions in history. They traveled close to 8,000 miles over the course of two years and four months and only lost one man, apparently due to appendicitis. During that time, they literally filled in the map of the western frontier and paved the way for the building of a nation in the newly acquired Louisiana Territory.

They were skirting the edge of myth and reality. Jefferson thought they might find blue-eyed Welsh-speaking Indians, Peruvian llamas, woolly mammoths or even giant ground sloths. Sergeant Gass wrote that he expected to confront "warlike savages of gigantic stature." Some of Jefferson's scholarly books proposed encounters with erupting volcanoes and even mountains of undissolved salt. Other readings led Jefferson to wonder if Virginia's Blue Ridge Mountains might be the continent's highest. In 1803, such myths defined the uncharted West. The Lewis and Clark expedition later dispelled the most widely held myth—the existence of a northwest passage, a coveted series of rivers connecting the Missouri to the Pacific, allowing an easily accessible trade route.

Thomas Jefferson believed such a discovery could break open the wealth of North America. Jefferson saw that the United States had the potential to become a powerful nation if it could add the area west of the Mississippi to its territory. He was a true visionary. Remember, he was pondering all of this at a time when only four roads crossed west of the Appalachian Mountains. By horse, it was impossible to get anything from the Mississippi to the Atlantic seaboard in less than six weeks. The answer in tapping the world marketplace seemed to be by following the Ohio, Missouri and Mississippi Rivers down to the Gulf of Mexico, or by finding a water route to the Pacific Ocean.

The Missouri River Then & Now

The Missouri River of 1804 was nothing like it is now. Lewis & Clark would probably not recognize the Missouri as the river they traversed 200 years ago. Today, we have a river with a main channel that is 300 yards wide and nine feet deep. It has been called America's fastest navigable river, rushing by at speeds of four to five miles an hour. That's fast. The river is more like a fast-moving drainage ditch than a biologically diverse river. Its primary role today is dwindling but still important river barge use.

The Missouri River of 1804 was a maze of dangerous snags, sandbars and collapsing banks. A wide, shallow, slow-moving wetland buffered the edges of its unpredictable and meandering main channel. It was a vast series of interconnected, braided streams, stretching more than a mile wide at places.

And the river was peppered with the stuff of a river captain's nightmares: collapsing riverbanks, shifting sandbars and menacing snags—downed trees with rootballs still intact, which had a nasty habit of lying submerged right below the water's surface. In Karl Bodmer's painting *Snags (Sunken Trees) on the Missouri,* the snags loom large and in chaotic multitudes, ready to thwart any attempts at navigation.

Clark wrote of one such snag near present-day Arrow Rock, "Stern Struck a log under Water & She Swung round on the Snag, with her broad Side to the Current," causing, "a disagreeable and Dangerous Situation, particularly as immense large trees were Drifting down and we lay imediately in their Course."

In other words, the expedition had to be ready for anything. Traveling such a river required various forms of propulsion. Poling and rowing were by far the most common ways of getting the boats upriver. Sails were used to a limited degree. Poling—pushing poles into the muck and pushing the boat upriver—was often employed when rapids threatened the unwieldy boats. Cordelling was also used. In cordelling, a sturdy rope is tied to the bow and the crew get in the river or on the bank and start pulling the boat upriver. Although this may

The river of 1804 was peppered with the stuff of a riverboat captain's nightmares: collapsing riverbanks, shifting sandbars and menacing snags.

sound extremely inefficient to modern readers, this was cutting edge military technology 200 years ago.

However, it wasn't long after the Voyage of Discovery that new technologies took hold on the Missouri. By 1819, the first steamboat was plying the Big Muddy. Steamboat traffic was vital to the opening of the West, reaching its peak in 1880. Steamboats shipped flour, salt, corn, tobacco and hemp downriver to the markets in St. Louis and beyond and returned laden with molasses, sugar, coffee and manufactured items.

For example, Rocheport, a Mid-Missouri rivertown, saw 57 steamboats make 500 landings in 1849 alone. The paddle wheeler's shallow draft eventually allowed rivermen to navigate their way upriver 2,285 miles from the mouth to Fort Benton, Montana.

Riverbottom mud dries out and cracks under the relentless summer sun.

The River Changed By the Hands of Man

The river has evolved both naturally and more dramatically by the hands of man. In a world that covets control, order and progress, the Missouri was a wild card. It was moody, erratic and unpredictable. It crept out of its banks and served no purpose for commercial navigation. So the Corps of Engineers built a new river where the Pekitanoui once flowed.

The Corps of Engineers began snag removal as early as 1824, with Congress appropriating funds specifically for Missouri River improvement beginning in 1881. But it was the Missouri River Bank Stabilization and Navigation Project, authorized by Congress in 1912, that established the beginning of a century-long project to create a permanent channel for navigation from St. Louis to Sioux City, Iowa.

The Corps started by removing snags—hundreds upon hundreds of them. Then they found that they could draw a straighter line on a map than a meandering river could cut. The Corps removed oxbows and straightened out the river, shortening the river by 57 miles just within the state of Missouri and a total of more than 125 miles before reaching Sioux City.

One of the most effective ways of channelizing the river was the building of wing dikes and piers into the river to divert the current away from the eroding shoreline. These structures increased the river's velocity, loosened sediment and deepened the channel. The Corps of Engineers shored up the banks with rock and they dredged. They built an amazingly efficient channel nine feet deep and 300 feet wide that now scours itself.

Yet, our country's progress quickly outpaced the slow transport offered by water. We moved on, building highways and creating cities away from waterways. With railroads and 18-wheelers, commerce on the river is now limited primarily to grain and fertilizer. Although river traffic never reached even a fraction of the projected amount, more than 1.5 million tons of commodities are moved by barge annually on the Missouri River—a drop in the bucket compared to the bustle found on the Mississippi River.

On the alert for everpresent logs that float down the river like lumbering landmines, Bob Plummer signals "all is clear ahead" for the tillerman. He sits astride the bow of the Discovery Expedition's replica of Lewis & Clark's keelboat.

The Missouri River Today

ow we are in the midst of the Bicentennial Commemoration of the Lewis & Clark Expedition and suddenly many people are paying attention again to that silent blue ribbon that wraps across the middle of the state. Many travelers are hoping to travel in the footsteps of Lewis & Clark, to envision a river as the explorers first saw it.

There is much to be enjoyed there even today and the bicentennial also allows us a moment to reflect on how much has changed. It has been written that more than 90-percent of the biodiversity once found in and along the Missouri River is gone. In large part, this is due to the fact that the river had essentially been separated from the floodplain. Nature loves muck as much as does a boy in his Sunday best. As slower moving backwaters were removed, important spawning grounds were destroyed. When the river was bottlenecked in, confined to a third of its historic floodplain, yearly flooding ceased. Flooding was largely controlled, turning swampy wetlands, which are great for fish, amphibians, reptiles and insects, into topsoil suitable for farming.

As the Corps of Discovery sojourned across 1804 Missouri, they noted deer in great numbers along the banks "skipping in every derection." Many of the diverse mammals noted in their journals in Missouri, such as the elk, buffalo and most of the black bear, are gone. The bright green and yellow Carolina Parakeets noted in Clark's journal, which once ranged from the Canadian border to the Gulf and from the Atlantic to the Rocky Mountains, are now extinct.

But much of the nature they observed and many of the panoramic views they beheld can still be appreciated today. The Corps of Discovery immediately fell in love with the lush green valleys, which certainly reminded the Kentuckians and Virginians of their own green rolling homeland. They recorded that wild roses hugged the banks, along with ripening berries and grapes. Paw paws were to be found in great abundance.

Journal entries read *"...land verry good...butifull a peas of land as ever I saw...one of the most beatifull and picteresk seens that I ever beheld..."*

The area north of Kansas City was noted in Clark's journal, dated Wednesday, July 4, 1804. It offers a good example of how awestruck the Captain was by the area's beauty:

...The Plains of this countrey are covered with a Leek Green Grass, well calculated for the sweetest and most norushing hay—interspersed with Cops of trees, Spreding ther lofty branchs over Pools Springs or Brooks of fine water. Groops of Shrubs covered with the most delicious froot is to be seen in every direction, and nature appears to have exerted herself to butify the Senery by the variety of flours raiseing Delicately... above the Grass, which Strikes & profumes the Sensation, and amuses the mind... throws it into Conjecturing the cause of So magnificent a Senery in a Country thus Situated far removed from the Sivilised world to be enjoyed by nothing but the Buffalo Elk Deer & Bear in which it abounds...

On the western edge of Missouri on July 3, 1804, the party reported for the first time seeing the North American beaver. As their trip continued west, they would see unimaginable numbers of beavers. The insatiable fashion craze for beaver hats triggered increased exploration and settlement over the next 30 years, often called the "Golden Age of the American Fur Trade." The fur trade also jumpstarted the growth of a small village called St. Louis.

Loosening the Grip of Man

The bottlenecked Missouri River devastated many communities and destroyed thousands of acres of farmland in the Great Flood of 1993—the worst flood in recorded history. Another major flood in 1995 caused further devastation. As a result, many state and federal agencies made it a top priority to reopen some areas of the historic floodplain to the Missouri River. These agencies include the National Fish and Wildlife Service of the Big Muddy Wildlife Area, the Corps of Engineers, the Missouri Department of Conservation and others.

In the past two decades, more than 88,000 acres of bottomland have been purchased by these agencies to allow the river room to breathe once again: to prevent communities from being flooded, to protect farms, to preserve habitat and to restore habitat for fish and wildlife that have been lost during a century of channelization efforts. Wetlands have slowly begun to be restored and bottomland timber has been planted. The Corps of Engineers has also allowed an historically active, shallow side chute to reopen. The channel has already become a spawning ground for the endangered pallid sturgeon.

So through history, policy changes, politics and progress, the Missouri River still flows. A river once entrusted to rivermen and explorers seeking to fill in gaps on the map is now largely a silent place where poets and painters keep watch. After practically turning our backs on it for a hundred years in our pursuit of progress, it has become, according to the Missouri Department of Conservation, Missouri's number one underused natural resource. Somehow, the longest river system in the United States—one of the greatest rivers in the world—manages to meander largely unnoticed across our state day in and day out. It's a feat that no magician could match.

Daily it slips unnoticed by more than 4.5 million Missourians who live within a few minutes drive of it, from St. Joseph to Kansas City to Columbia and on to St. Charles and St. Louis. And yet in this information age, we know so little about it. Generally the only time it makes the news is when it's at floodstage and it has stretched beyond where we think its banks should be.

Perhaps the river is largely forgotten because the beauty of the Missouri River valley is so sublime. It rewards idle moments of contemplation as the sun crashes into the horizon in a fiery blaze, trailing stripped skies of vivid blue hues and subtle pinks. But the river doesn't take your breath away in an instant like the first time you see the Rocky Mountains. The beauty of the Missouri comes on slowly as the light shifts and the geese alight. The beauty here lies in its perfect painter's palette of saturated blues and greens. The beauty lies in the silence. Thousands of cubic feet of river and sediment plow by every minute with the force of a thousand freight trains, yet the river is quieter than a sleeping infant.

In addition to beauty, the other thing the Missouri River offers our frontierless age is solace. The Missouri is a place where we can reconnect with nature, with our own wildness, with the revering gaze of yesterday's explorers, and with our country's prodigious past. The river gives the soul a place to breathe. It is a place for imaginations to expand. A place where nature still reigns supreme, with horizons undisturbed by structures and banks unencumbered by our suburban endurance race of materialism.

On the Big Muddy, whether you look upstream or down, the river appears to stretch to infinity. It reaches all the way to the horizon. Some days it is as gray as a city park pigeon on an overcast day. Other days the river is bluer than a newborn baby's eyes. And on many days, if you strain your eyes to that distant point on the horizon, where the line blurs between river and sky, the river stretches right up to the limits of land until it kisses the sky and they dissolve into one.

And I think that's what draws the poets, the paddlers, the bird watchers, the hunters and the fisherman. In a measured world, the river is one of those things that seem to go on forever. It's wild. Relentless. Never ending. And it intends to stay that way.

So despite being channelized, bottlenecked and largely forgotten, the Missouri River has a future that looks bright. Although the debate about the future of the Missouri River rages on, I like the river flowing past my door. Sometimes it moves grain, which helps the farmers and reduces traffic on the highway. Some of the bottomlands are tilled—a veritable black gold—generating America's breadbasket. Some of the bottoms near my home have been purchased by various agencies to allow that important interchange between land and water—the wetlands—to take hold once again. There I see reason to hope for fewer floods and perhaps the return of a river more like what Lewis & Clark experienced. A wilder Missouri River.

Like Thoreau once said, "In wildness is the preservation of the world." With that return to wildness has come the resurgence of several endangered species, such as the national symbol of strength, the bald eagle. And as those wetlands become more overgrown and wild, those places will beckon to me. They will need to be explored, I am sure, with my young son.

River of Opportunity

Explore The Rivers of Lewis & Clark
By Canoe, By Barge, By Bike, By Train, By Air

Today's Missouri River offers many exciting ways to explore the Lewis & Clark Trail. As the Bicentennial Commemoration of Lewis & Clark's 1804 – 1806 voyage gets underway, it's incredible how few people venture out on the Missouri River. In fact, you could argue that the Missouri River valley (the river and its banks) is the least trod ground in Missouri.

Travel on the river that gave the state its name. Here we are in the state where Lewis & Clark for all practical purposes began and ended their trip. The Missouri River was Lewis & Clark's superhighway to the West. Yet today, although many people enjoy Missouri River views, few realize the countless ways to enjoy and to interact with the Missouri River valley.

The Missouri River has developed what I call the Grand Canyon Syndrome. That is, people drive up to see it, get out of their air-conditioned cars and photograph it. Perhaps they walk along its banks for a bit, but then they get back in their cars and move on to the next spot. Been there, done that.

The bicentennial offers a golden opportunity for people to not only reconnect with the Missouri River valley, but the Missouri River itself. Today, perhaps more than at any other time in the past 200 years, save for the riverboat days, there are more ways for landlocked Missourians to explore the Lewis & Clark Trail.

For so many years the river has taken a back seat to our rush for progress. And so, it only seems appropriate, that in this time of uncertainty, that nature would regain its prominent place in our psyche. There are many opportunities available for those wanting to explore the Missouri River, to see the river from the exact same vantage point as Lewis & Clark. And after all, you can't say you've done the Lewis & Clark Trail if you haven't gotten your feet wet. That trail is the Missouri River.

Everyone is busy with the phrase "Lewis & Clark Stood Here." Sort of odd, considering they were moving by water. The river is where their greatest mishaps and also most serene moments occurred.

Perhaps instead of using the phrase "Lewis & Clark Stood Here," it would be more beneficial if the slogan of Missouri's Bicentennial were "Lewis & Clark Rowed Here." After all, even the Division of Tourism's theme of "Missouri: Where the Rivers Run," seems an apt nod that the rivers are where it's at. If the Missouri motto were "Lewis & Clark Rowed Here," we could blanket both banks with spots that would suddenly gain much needed notoriety for the river. Photo ops would increase immeasurably.

Explore the
Missouri River

*T*he Missouri River demands respect. It is a big river. However, with the proper safety precautions, it offers a front row seat to the Lewis & Clark Trail that cannot be found anywhere else. Whether you are looking for a comfortable seat aboard a river barge, a tour aboard a small motorboat, the ease of a bus or the breeze to be found on a bike or in a canoe, there has never been more fun ways to explore this "River of Opportunity."

Explore the River By Canoe

P addling the Missouri River will change your view of the river forever. No other river experience allows you the solitude and up-close-and-personal view of the river. Several communities may offer canoe or raft rentals soon. Only experienced paddlers who understand the unique nature of the Missouri River should get on the river without someone who has experience on the river. Exploring the river by canoe with experienced paddlers is something you'll never forget. Most first-time paddlers on the Missouri are surprised that the river feels more like a slow-moving lake than a fast-moving big river.

There are several great resources for boating and paddling the Missouri River: the *Lewis & Clark Bicentennial Lower Missouri River Guide to Recreation and Visitors Safety;* the *Corps of Engineers River Charts;* and the *Paddler's Guide to Missouri.* These are available by calling the Pebble Publishing Bookstore at (800) 576-7322. Visit them in Rocheport or go online to www.pebblepublishing.com.

Explore the River By Barge & John Boat

A comparatively new option for exploring the Missouri River is operated by RiverBarge Excursion Lines, Inc. RiverBarge offers the most stately option for experiencing the Big Muddy without getting your toes wet. Ride aboard the 198-guest, 730-foot long *R/B River Explorer,* the only hotel barge traveling America's inland waterways. Offering a complete vacation package, "Barging Through America" allows guests to experience the river while also getting ample opportunities to visit rivertowns along the way.

Onboard historians, regional entertainers, homestyle cooking, a family atmosphere and comfortable amenities make this a popular option for exploring the Missouri River Valley. Tours offered ply the river between St. Louis and Kansas City. Another trip travels from Kansas City upriver to Sioux City, Iowa. A nine-day excursion from St. Charles to Kansas City,

Paddling past the Manitou Bluffs near Rocheport, Missouri.

called the "Voyage of Discovery," is scheduled for 2004. Another trip scheduled for fall 2004 is the "Show Me the Big Muddy." Read the article "Rolling on the River," in the June/July 2001 issue of *Missouri Life*.

(888) GO BARGE • www.riverbarge.com

Big River Tours, based out of Lexington, offers half-day and all-day small boat tours of six people or less on the Missouri River in central and western Missouri. Tours include picnic cruises, Kansas City cruises, Big Muddy National Fish and Wildlife Refuge cruises, Fort Osage daytrips, evening cruises and more. Visit their website or call for more information.

(816) 470-3206 • www.bigrivertours.com

Visit the 350-year-old burr oak tree in McBaine, near Columbia, either by car or by bike, when touring the Katy Trail.

Explore the Trail By Bike on the Katy Trail

Missourians are also able to explore in the footsteps of Lewis & Clark along the Katy Trail State Park. Stretching across the state for more than 225 miles, this hiking and biking trail meanders within view of the Missouri River for much of the trail's distance across the state, allowing you to enjoy the longest public, non-motorized portion of the entire Lewis & Clark Trail.

The solitude, scenery and quaint small towns dotting the trail's edge make the Katy Trail a popular daytrip and weekend destination. Plan to average about 8 – 12 miles per hour on your bike. Most cyclists that ride the trail from end to end allow themselves five days for a comfortable trip. Popular Katy Trail trailheads rich with Lewis & Clark history include the trail's easternmost trailhead, St. Charles, heading west all the way to Boonville. The Missouri Department of Natural Resources offers an annual organized Katy Trail ride, complete with vehicle support. Visit their website listed below for more information.

Another book that would be immensely helpful for those planning a Lewis & Clark Trail trip in Missouri is *The Complete Katy Trail Guidebook,* which offers detailed information for all of the towns and stops along the entire 225-mile Katy Trail.

This guidebook includes up-to-date descriptions of the services to be found, places to stay, mile markers, camping, area history, and maps along with a ton of photographs.

Call Pebble Publishing at (800) 576-7322, visit their Rocheport bookstore or go to www.pebblepublishing.com.

For more information about the Katy Trail State Park, call (800) 334-6946.
www.katytrailstatepark.com
katytrail.showmestate.com

Did you know that the Bed & Breakfast Inns of Missouri Association has links to B&Bs all along the Lewis & Clark Trail? Check it out: www.bbim.org.

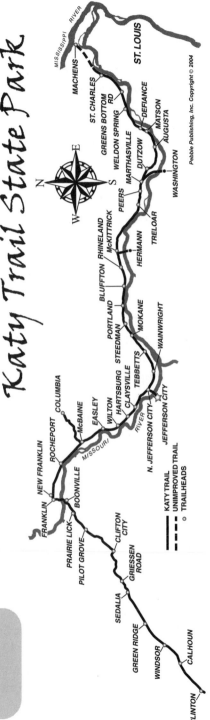

Explore the Trail By Train

Seeing the countryside whirr by while enjoying the comfort and nostalgia of traveling the world by train is another great way to explore the Lewis & Clark Trail in Missouri. Amtrak has stops at several major communities along the Missouri River. Step on in St. Louis (Kirkwood), or Kansas City and disembark at or near rivertowns including Washington, Hermann, Jefferson City and Independence. Special vacation packages and summer rates make this option an affordable experience for the whole family. Discounts for students and seniors are available.

(800) USA-RAIL • www.amtrak.com

Explore the Trail By Bus

For those not looking for a river-based experience, there are also several groups that offer bus tours of the many small rivertowns that dot the banks of the Missouri and Mississippi Rivers. Check your local phone book under tour operator, or call a local travel agent for more information. Central Travel in Jefferson City offers several such tours.

(800) 282-9945 • www.centraltravel.vacation.com
(800) 492-2593 • www.missourilife.com

Explore the Trail By Air

If only Lewis & Clark had been offered such a vantage point to see what was ahead! As you plan your Lewis & Clark Trail trip across Missouri, be sure to stop in at local airports to inquire if they offer airplane rides. Many riverside communities, such as Washington and Boonville, offer short airplane rides that are affordable and unforgettable. Call the Washington Airport at (636) 433-5454 and inquire about their rides for two. Appointments are required. Another way to view the slender ribbon of river from above is to look in the yellow pages for area balloon rides.

Commonly Asked
Lewis & Clark
Trail Questions

How many miles of river did Lewis & Clark traverse in present-day Missouri?

They advanced 195 miles up the Mississippi River in 1803 traveling to their winter camp at Wood River, Illinois. They then traversed nearly 600 additional miles across the state by way of the Missouri River in 1804.

How many days did the Corps of Discovery spend in Missouri?

The Corps of Discovery spent 66 days in the present-day state of Missouri, where they rarely made more than 12 miles of progress a day. To Missouri's great fortune, Lewis and Clark started measuring their course and distance at the mouth of the Ohio River. This allows us to re-create with James Harlan's meticulously researched maps the progress of Lewis & Clark. According to Harlan, there were 70 outward-bound (1803 – 1804) campsites adjacent to or within the present state of Missouri, and 51 of these sites were calculated to fall within the present boundaries of Missouri, with nine in Illinois, seven in Kansas and three in Nebraska.

Has the Missouri River changed much in 200 years?

Today the Missouri River we see is essentially like a horse that has been broken to ride. It's almost impossible to fathom the difference in the river from 1804 and now. Read "The Missouri River Then & Now" on page 20. The Corps of Discovery had many moments where the river and gusting winds joined forces to pummel the crew's best efforts. Read Clark's entry for July 14, 1804 (on page 220). Clark's journal during their trip across Missouri is riddled with mentions of "the worst place I have seen." See also page 157.

Has the Missouri River always been muddy?

Clark offers an answer to that question on page 169.

What's your favorite journal entry written by Clark during their trip up the Missouri River?

My favorite Clark entry was written on July 4, 1804 (see page 200). His writing not only recorded the crew's celebration of Independence Day, but some of his most eloquent writing on the beauty of the Missouri River valley. He writes, "nature appears to have exerted herself to butify the Senery by the variety of flours raiseing Delicately and highly... above the Grass, which Strikes & profumes the Sensation, and amuses the mind throws it into Conjecturing the cause of So magnificent a Senerey... in a Country thus Situated far removed from the Sivilised world to be enjoyed by nothing but the Buffalo Elk Deer & Bear in which it abounds."

If I only have a few days to travel the trail in Missouri, what are a few popular stops to make?

Now there's a loaded question! There are so many unique sites worth visiting that they easily filled up all of the pages of this book! A few of my favorites are: St. Charles, St. Louis' Missouri History Museum, Hermann, Washington, Bonnot's Mill, Clark's Hill State Historic Site, Lupus, Rocheport, Arrow Rock State Park, Fort Osage, Kansas City's Case Park and Steamboat Arabia, Parkville, Weston Bend State Park, St. Joseph's Sunset Grill and Atchison, Kansas to name a few. Take a thorough read of this book and you will certainly find many more excellent destinations too!

A want to stand exactly where Clark stood. Do you have any suggestions on places I should go?

Clark's Hill State Historic Site near Jefferson City (see page 122), Fort Osage National Historic Landmark (see page 174), and Kansas City's Case Park (see page 181).

What was the general reaction to the return of the Corps of Discovery almost two and a half years after they first set out?

On September 17, 1806, as the Corps of Discovery traveled back downriver a group they meet was "somewhat astonished to See us return and appeared rejoiced to meet us... we had been long Since given out by the people of the US... and almost forgotten, the President of the U. States had yet hopes of us..."

Exploring
Lewis & Clark's
Missouri

Westward Bound

November 20, 1803 – July 18, 1804

What follows are excerpts from Clark's journals as the expedition slowly worked its way across the area we now know as the state of Missouri. Highlights of the journal entries are included, as well as modern-day stops along the trail that will interest those following in their footsteps.

Refer to page 224 to read William Clark's journal excerpts from their return trip in 1806. After reaching the Pacific Ocean and re-crossing the West, they returned downriver and re-entered the state of Missouri on September 9, 1806. The expedition was completed in St. Louis on September 23, 1806.

Region Review

Journey Up the Mississippi River

Fall of 1803

Lewis & Clark camped near Cairo, Illinois, from November 14 to 19, 1803, at the confluence of the Ohio and Mississippi Rivers. On November 20, 1803, the Corps began their ascent of the Mississippi River.

From there, they followed the Mississippi River— the eastern border of the present-day state of Missouri—to where they would construct their winter camp at Camp Dubois, near Wood River, Illinois. They arrived at Camp Dubois on December 12, 1803.

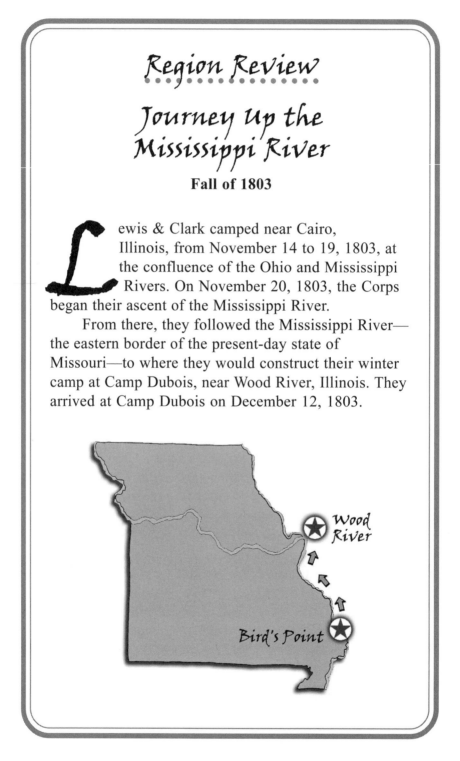

Wood River

Bird's Point

Today's Trail
Explore Fort Massac State Park
Metropolis, Illinois

Here, on November 11, 1803, Lewis hired the journey's interpreter George Drouillard, at a pay rate of $25 per month. Despite the captain's inability to properly spell his name in their entries, Drouillard became one of the most valuable members of the expedition, due to his sharp hunting skills. Overlooking the Ohio River from the southern tip of Illinois, Fort Massac became Illinois's first state park in 1908. The French built Fort de l'Ascension on the site in 1757, during the French and Indian War, when France and Great Britain were fighting for ultimate control of central North America. Rebuilt in 1759 – 60, the structure was renamed Massac. Rich with historical significance, it has come under fire only once. Actual re-creations of pioneer life of the 1700s during the annual Fort Massac Encampment and several living history weekends each year bring the past to life, letting you experience it yourself.

(618) 524-4712 • dnr.state.il.us

Today's Trail
Explore Bird's Point, Missouri

Lewis & Clark first set foot on land of the Louisiana Territory (part of which would become the state of Missouri) during their stay from November 14 to 19, 1803, when they camped on the southern tip of Illinois. On one or more occasions, expedition members crossed the Mississippi River at what is now Bird's Point, making this the site of the expedition's first entry into what would become our state of Missouri.

Bird's Point was the first settlement in Mississippi County, and it dates back to Spanish land grants. The river landing was bought by Abram Bird in 1805 and the place was named for him. His descendants still own that land today. On an old ledger kept by the warehouse and general store at Bird's Point, the name is written in various ways. It appears as Bird's Landing, Illinois Point and Bird's Point.

November 22, 1803

Expedition Entry
Near Commerce, Missouri
November 22, 1803

    Lewis kills a heath hen to make soup for Clark, who has been ill for nearly a week. They see part of an American settlement of about 15 families in a bottom called Tywappity. About 22 miles above the confluence with the Ohio River, the men overtake two keelboats from Louisville, Kentucky, that are loaded with dry goods and whiskey and bound for Kaskaskia, Illinois. The Corps of Discovery records seeing the first poplar and white oak since they've been on the Mississippi River, as well as the tallest scouring rush plant observed anywhere—one stalk is more than eight feet high and three inches in circumference. After they camp on the eastern shore, crew member Nathaniel Pryor goes out to hunt and does not return. To help bring him in, the men fire guns and blow a horn, to no avail.

A diary entry from 1857 recounts an early Mississippi River crossing

This morning we ferried the largest river on the North American Continent [the Mississippi River], and it is well calculated to fill the mind and soul with awe and reverance, when we remember the Hand that formed this stupendous river formed also the smallest grain of matter in the Universe. It is indeed a grand sight to see the noble steamboats gliding on its rolling current, and just to think of the 1,000 people that are constantly being conveyed on its mighty waters, and at the solemn thought that thousands are sleeping their last sleep on its bottom! How these thoughts conspire to make us remember our own feebleness and entire dependence on the Mercies of God... the Mississippi bottom is the richest land I ever saw... nearly entirely in woods... The trees on this bottom are the tallest and largest I ever saw and suppose not many larger in the world. It makes me grow dizzy to look up to their tops... by Martha Woods.

Around 1733, French soldier Jean Girardot was traveling through the area and found a rock promontory overlooking the Mississippi. He decided it was a good place to station his trading post. It sat on what is now called "Cape Rock," and what was later to become Cape Girardeau.

Expedition Entry
Site of present-day Cape Girardeau
November 23, 1803

Pryor still has not returned. The men fire guns, blow the horn again and then they leave without him. They pass Cape La Croix Creek, land at Cape Girardeau, and call on the commandant there, Louis Lorimier. Lewis attends a horse race with Lorimier and his family. In a dispute over the race, Lorimier loses four horses worth two hundred dollars. The scene reminds Lewis of uncivilized backwoodsmen in Kentucky. Lewis wrote, "It is not extrawdinary that these people should be disorderly they are almost entirely emegrant from the fronteers of Kentuckey & Tennessee, and are the most dessolute and abandoned even among these people; they are men of desperate fortunes, but little to loose either character or property—they bett very high on these raises in proportion to their wealth."

Today's Trail

Explore Cape Girardeau, Missouri

Located 120 miles south of St. Louis on the Mississippi River, Cape Girardeau began as a tiny French trading post. It evolved from a frontier settlement to a present-day community of 40,000 residents. Two men were essential in the founding of Cape Girardeau. The first was French soldier Jean Girardot. In about 1733, he was traveling through and found a rock promontory overlooking the Mississippi. He decided it was a good place for his trading post. It sat on what is now called Cape Rock. At the time, more than 20 Indian tribes lived in the area. Trappers and river travelers soon discovered this bit of civilization carved out of a vast forest. They called the place Cape Girardot. Girardot, being a frontiersman and trader at heart, soon moved on in search of other discoveries.

In 1793, Louis Lorimier, a noted trader, was commissioned by the Spanish governor general to establish a military post in Cape Girardot from which to trade and interact with the Indians. The post, called the Red House, was built on the site of the present-day Old St. Vincent's Church. Red House was a center of government and a place of trade with the Shawnee and Delaware Indians. Although some called the settlement Lorimont after Lorimier, the name Cape Girardot stuck and was later corrupted to its present form.

Under Lorimier's intelligent government and leadership, the settlement grew. In 1803, the region became an American possession because of the Louisiana Purchase. The cost for the land was two cents an acre, and Lorimier donated four acres for the establishment of a seat of justice. In 1806, the city was plotted and incorporated in 1808.

With the arrival of the steamboat in 1835, Cape Girardeau became a river boomtown, the busiest port between St. Louis and Memphis. Until the Civil War, the riverfront was a busy commercial hub where many steamboat travelers disembarked.

Be sure to visit the Cape Girardeau riverfront area. The Missouri Wall of Fame is a creative and fun way to make use of the flood wall near the historic downtown (yes, they included local celebrity Rush Limbaugh!). The immense flood wall has high-water marks. Imagine standing there at the railroad tracks in six feet of water in 1844 and 1943. In 1973, you would have been standing in about ten feet of water and more than 15 feet of water in 1993.

Tour the Cape River Heritage Museum. Located in the old Fire Station, this museum displays river-related artifacts and historical items. The Cape Girardeau Convention & Visitors Bureau is located at the corner of Main Street and Broadway, right next to the riverfront. (800) 777-0068.

The Courthouse in Cape's historic downtown area.

Leave time after dinner to watch the sun set while walking the riverfront trail.

The N'Orleans Restaurant in Cape Girardeau is a great place to eat in the heart of the historic downtown area.

While in the area, head west to visit scenic Burfordville to tour the scenic Bollinger Mill State Historic Site. See corn being ground into meal by water power—just as it was done long ago. The covered bridge nearby, dated to 1858, is the oldest of only four remaining covered bridges in Missouri.

(573) 243-4591 • www.mostateparks.com/bollinger.htm

Artist rendering of the Red House Interpretive Center by Margaret Randol Dement.

Today's Trail

Explore the Red House, Lorimier's Home & Trading Post
Cape Girardeau, Missouri

Constructed by the Cape Girardeau Lewis & Clark Bicentennial Commission with the help of local volunteers, the Red House Interpretive Center was designed to commemorate the visit of Lewis & Clark in November of 1803.

The interpretive center's exhibits reflect the lives of the early settlers of the "Old Cape Girardeau District." In addition, a rendering of the Louis Lorimier Trading Post displays authentic items that would have been sold during the period. Tours can be arranged by contacting the convention and visitors bureau at (800) 777-0068.

Don Louis Lorimier, Cape Girardeau's founder, welcomed the expedition members at the original Red House, when the Corps of Discovery stopped there on November 23, 1803. The explorers were on their way to their winter camp on the Illinois side of the river at Camp Dubois, opposite St. Louis.

When Lewis first arrived, Lorimier was not home and Lewis was directed to a nearby horse race, where Lorimier was wagering mightily.

Meriwether Lewis wrote four pages in his diary about *Cape Jerado,* Louis Lorimier and his Shawnee wife, the colorful residents (see page 43), the events that transpired here and Lorimier's "handsome" daughter, whom Lewis describes as "the most descent looking female I have seen since I left the settlement in Kentucky."

The Red House sits on the site of the Old St. Vincent's Church. An archaeological dig of the site is in the works. Be sure to visit the reconstructed Red House.

(573) 335-1631 • (800) 777-0068
capegirardeaucvb.org/bicentennial.html

Opposite page: The Trail of Tears State Park sign portrays Native Americans during their forced relocation in the winter of 1838-39.

Names To Know
Louis Lorimier

Lorimier, along with Jean Girardot, is credited with founding Cape Girardeau. He came to the area in 1793 after being commissioned by the Spanish to establish a military post for trade and interaction with American Indians. Lorimier is also thought by many historians to be the uncle of Corps of Discovery interpreter and civilian guide George Drouillard.

Lewis describes the physical characteristics of Lorimier including his extraordinary hair. Standing at approximately 5 feet 8 inches, this dark-skinned, dark-eyed and dark-haired, French-born entrepreneur boasted a mane of hair that would be spoken of for generations to come. According to Lewis' journals, Lorimier accounted that his dark, well-kept tresses were "long enough at one point that they touched the ground when he was standing erect."

Expedition Entry
Near Neely's Landing, Missouri
November 24, 1803

As the explorers set out in the morning, they are hailed by Pryor, who is ill and fatigued after being lost for two days. Lewis observes limestone rocks embedded with chunks of chert.

Today's Trail
Explore Trail of Tears State Park
Near Fruitland, Missouri

A stunning view of the Mississippi River can be found at the Trail of Tears State Park. The 3,415-acre park is a memorial to a tragic event in America's history. Under orders of President Andrew Jackson, five tribes of southeastern Indians were relocated to reservations in Oklahoma. They included the Creek, Chickasaw, Choctaw, Seminole and Cherokee. More than 16,000 were forced out against their will. In winter 1838 – 39, an endless procession of wagons, horsemen and people on foot traveled the 800 miles west to Indian Territory. The park is on the site where nine of 13 groups of Cherokee Indians crossed

Trail of Tears State Park offers a panoramic view of the Mississippi.

the Mississippi River during the harsh winter of 1838 – 39. The Indians endured brutal conditions: rain, snow, freezing cold, hunger and disease. Floating ice hindered many attempted river crossings. In the end, more than 4,000 Cherokees lost their lives on the march. The visitors center interprets the forced relocation and the park's natural features. Hiking trails that wind along the bluffs allow you to ponder this sad story, while you enjoy the area's serene beauty that belies its past. A 10-mile trail accesses more remote areas of the park. A Mississippi River boat ramp, a swimming beach at Lake Boutin, fishing and camping are available here too.

(573) 334-1711 • www.mostateparks.com/trailoftears.htm

Expedition Entry
Near Wittenberg, Missouri
November 25, 1803

The men come to Apple Creek, which is the largest stream they've seen yet. They arrive at Grand Tower (now known as Tower Rock), just before sunset and camp on the Missouri shore.

Expedition Entry

Grand Tower (now known as Tower Rock)
November 26, 1803

Lewis climbs this limestone formation (now known as Tower Rock) and drops a cord from the top to determine that it is 92 feet high. On the Missouri side, a high point of land topped by a conical, "sugar loaf" formation looks down on the tower and affords a beautiful view of the river. Another large rock located in the river 300 yards from this point is 120 yards in circumference and 40 feet high. Lewis speculates that these outcroppings form part of a ridge that was 200 feet high and ran across the river and was eroded over time. Lewis notes that when the river is high, a powerful whirlpool forms between the Grand Tower and a nearby rock formation.

Today's Trail

Explore Tower Rock Natural Area
Near Wittenberg, Missouri

When Lewis & Clark came by Tower Rock in 1803, Lewis reported that travelers on the Mississippi River regarded Tower Rock in much the same way as sailors viewed crossing the equator. Tradition held that rivermen passing Tower Rock for the first time must either furnish spirits to drink or be dunked.

The 32-acre Tower Rock Natural Area is located in Perry County, 1.5 miles south of Wittenberg. The area offers a scenic view of the tower, however the island itself is only accessible by boat. You can walk on flat rocks near river level or climb a bluff near Tower Rock for better views. (573) 290-5730.

Flows around the island can be dangerous. Back in 1839, a couple married on the rock. The wedding party of 10 was departing when their boat was caught in a whirlpool. Only a slave who clung to the boat survived.

Low waters in February of 2003 allowed visitors the rare opportunity to walk to Tower Rock, normally accessible only by boat.

Tower Rock Rooted in River Legend & Lore

T ower Rock juts out of the slow muddy waters of the Mississippi River about a hundred miles south of St. Louis. On November 26, 1803, Meriwether Lewis climbed this limestone formation and dropped a cord from the top to determine that it was 92 feet high.

One reporter called it a "colossal tree stump." To me, it looks more like a mini-me version of Wyoming's Devil's Tower, featured in the movie *Close Encounters of the Third Kind.* It juts like a limestone mesa out of the Mississippi River about 300 feet off the riverbank in Perry County, Missouri. This unique eminence has been known over the years as Tower Rock, Grand Tower, Grand Tower Roc and La Roche de la Croix.

A knob of rock this size (the roughly flat summit is approximately three quarters of an acre) would probably not even be afforded a second glance in someplace like the Badlands, but along the Mississippi River, it's an anomaly that has attracted awe, fear and even ownership disputes. As one author wrote, "Tower Rock has the paradoxical distinction of being both unique and unremarkable. There is nothing else like it along the Mississippi, yet from the point of view of geologists, it is merely an erosional remnant, not appreciably different from many others across the face of the globe, that (for reasons they do not attempt to explain) was overlooked by the river as it ground away the surrounding rock."

Tower Rock has played a prominent role in rivermen's psyches for centuries. It played a role much like crossing the Equator. Upon first crossing past the Tower Rock, new deckhands would either have to furnish spirits or be dunked.

Pere Jacques Marquette paddled by Tower Rock in 1673. In his journal, he wrote that it is "a place that is dreaded by the savages because they believe the Manitou is there, that is to say, a demon that devours travelers."

Perhaps the superstition had its roots in truth, since a dangerous eddy forms between the rock and the shore during high water. That dangerous eddy at one time in the 1800s even drowned an entire wedding party, after capsizing their boat after the bride and groom exchanged vows on the rock.

During the summer of 2003, the river level fell so low that for only the second time in the memory of local residents the stone shelf between the rock and the mainland was left dry and visitors could walk out to it. The rock became an instant attraction.

Some believe Tower Rock is the nation's smallest national park. That theory was widely spread by Robert Ripley in his book *Believe It or Not* in 1933. That myth has been perpetuated in a notation on the Corps of Engineers' river navigation chart.

Not so, says Edwin Bearss, chief historian for the National Park Service in Washington. "President Ulysses S. Grant had the distinction of signing the first national park legislation. But it was to create Yellowstone National Park in 1872."

November 27, 1803

Expedition Entry
Near Chester, Illinois
November 27, 1803

The crew sets out before sunrise and proceeds to a point of rocks on the edge of a long range of hills on the Missouri side. A quarter mile away is another creek, Cinque Hommes Creek, which is 20 miles long and home to a considerable number of settlers and as many as three grist mills.

Today's Trail
Explore Seventy Six Conservation Area

Seventy Six Conservation Area is located in extreme eastern Perry County at the end of Route D. The area covers 818 acres of forest and borders a two-mile section of the Mississippi River. A long and winding trail leads to a nice river overlook. Bank and wing dike fishing are both good ways to catch catfish and carp here.

Expedition Entry
Near Sainte Genevieve, Missouri
November 28, 1803

Lewis leaves Clark in charge of the boats. Clark and the men set out from Horse Island, opposite Kaskaskia River. A thick fog obscures view of the shore. They pass Donohoe's Landing on the Missouri side, where boats receive salt from the nearby saline licks that would eventually make the community of Ste. Genevieve prosperous.

They pass the mouth of Saline Creek, which has a "thick settlement" of pioneers on its banks. After passing swift water between sandbars, the men arrive at the landing opposite Old Ste. Genevieve known as Kaskaskia.

Today's Trail

Explore Sainte Genevieve, Missouri

Nowhere in Missouri is the historic mix of cultures along the Mississippi as readily visible to visitors as in Ste. Genevieve. "Ste. Gen" was founded in 1735 by French Canadians who followed Pere Marquette, Joliet and LaSalle down the Mississippi to settle the Illinois Country. Ste. Genevieve contains the largest number of surviving French Colonial houses in the United States. Numerous sites are open to visitors, some of which are early vertical log cabins—the preferred construction method of settlers here. Start your visit at the information office at 66 S. Main (corner of Main & Market).

A full day in Ste. Genevieve begins with breakfast in one of the town's charming B&Bs or hotels. Elegant B&B options are numerous. The Steiger Haus B&B specializes in murder mysteries, with several offered every week, call (573) 883-5881.

In the morning, visit the Great River Road Interpretive Center to watch the Ste. Genevieve video. A walking tour tape is available at several B&Bs and at the information office. The tour of museum houses begins with the elegant Maison Guibourd Valle house at Fourth and Merchant. The next stop is the museum and then the Felix Valle House State Historic Site. The home tour also visits the Bolduc and Bolduc-LeMeilleur houses operated by the Missouri Chapter of Colonial Dames. Visit the Amoureaux House to view a wonderful scale model of the community, circa 1830. Across the road are the bottoms that were cultivated by the early farmers, who plowed in long, narrow strips from river to bluff.

Be sure to visit Kaskaskia Island, Illinois—reachable only through Missouri—to see the church and the Kaskaskia Bell, gifted in 1740 by King Louis XV. Be sure to hear their Lewis & Clark story. The kids will enjoy taking the nearby ferry across the Mississippi. Tour nearby Fort de Chartres, enjoy the underground boat ride at Bonne Terre Mine, hike in beautiful Hawn State Park and learn about Missouri's lead belt at Missouri Mines State Historic Site.

(800) 373-7007 • www.saintegenevievetourism.org

November 28, 1803

To∂ay's Trail

Explore Crown Valley Winery
Near Sainte Genevieve, Missouri

A short drive from Ste. Gen will bring you to the Crown Valley Winery, one of the largest up-and-coming wineries in the state. Enjoy a country setting on the shaded decks or find a new favorite wine at one of the indoor tasting bars. A catwalk-style building allows visitors a chance to peer down upon a sea of stainless steel cooling tanks—putting you right in the midst of the winemaking process. The 40,000-square-foot building houses the complete winery production process, from crush pad through automated bottling equipment. Tours of the vineyards and the winemaking process are available. There is also a gift shop and a deli. Check the website for music performances, festival weekends and information on wine classes. Contact the Ste. Genevieve tourism office for information on other area wineries that you don't want to miss: (800) 373-7007.

(573) 756-9463 • www.crownvalleywinery.com

Crown Valley's chief winemaker "thieves" a sample of an aging dry red straight out of the oak barrel. Note to self: write more guidebooks that involve winery stops.

Expedition Entry
Kaskaskia, Illinois
November 28 – December 2, 1803

When Lewis and Clark arrived in Kaskaskia, Illinois, on November 28, 1803, Fort Kaskaskia was the most northwest military post of the United States. Located on the eastern bank of the Mississippi River, 60 miles south of St. Louis, Fort Kaskaskia was home to Captain Russell Bissell's infantry company and Captain Amos Stoddard's artillery company. The first thing Meriwether Lewis did upon arrival was to show the captains his orders from Secretary of War Henry Dearborn. The orders gave Lewis an open invitation to acquire the volunteers and supplies he needed from the post.

Twelve men were recruited from Fort Kaskaskia, six from Captain Bissell's infantry company and five from Captain Stoddard's artillery company. They included Sgt. John Ordway and privates Peter Weiser, Richard Windsor, Patrick Gass, John Boley and John Collins. Gass proved invaluable on the expedition due to his carpentry skills and was promoted to sergeant during the expedition. Others recruited included John Dame, John Robertson, Ebeneezer Tuttle, Isaac White and Alexander Hamilton Willard.

At this point, there is a gap in the journals. Apparently, Clark remains in the Ste. Genevieve–Kaskaskia area and then resumes the upriver journey with the crew on December 3, while Lewis stays behind until December 5 to attend to necessary meetings and to complete some paperwork. He then travels by horseback to Cahokia. From this point, Clark makes all journal entries until April of 1805.

December 3, 1803

Today's Trail

Explore Fort Kaskaskia State Historic Site
Ellis Grove, Illinois

Fort Kaskaskia is situated on a bluff overlooking the Mississippi River and offers scenic views of the American Bottoms, the confluence of the Mississippi and Kaskaskia Rivers, and the site of the original town of Kaskaskia, which was once the first state capitol of Illinois. While in the area, be sure to also visit the nearby Pierre Menard Home State Historic Site. Call (618) 859-3741.

At the time of Lewis & Clark's visit, 467 people lived in Kaskaskia. With its location along the Mississippi and at the mouth of the Kaskaskia River, the town grew into an important mercantile center. The Kaskaskia settlement grew as western expansion took off. In 1809, the territory of Illinois was formed, with Kaskaskia as its capital. In fact, the village was the first capital of Illinois when it became a state on December 3, 1818.

Due to major flooding in 1881, the Mississippi started to change its course, gouging out a new channel in the Kaskaskia River, which created an island where the old village was located. Further devastation occurred in 1993. Today, only about 300 residents remain.

Expedition Entry
December 3 – 4, 1803

Clark and his men leave before sunrise and come to the Missouri shore after dark. The next day, they pass Gabourie Creek at the mouth of a landing for trading boats of Ste. Genevieve, a small town of about 120 French families that is situated on the spurs of the highland. The men press on and see a cave 12 feet in diameter and 70 feet above the water. They pass the site of Old Fort de Chartres.

Today's Trail
Explore Fort de Chartres
Prairie du Rocher, Illinois

Fort de Chartres was the site of a series of fortresses built by the French with construction beginning in the early 1700s and lasting through 1760. Its walls, 15 feet high and three feet thick, enclosed approximately four acres. French officials named it in honor of Louis duc de Chartres, son of the regent of France. The site was the center of French control in the Illinois Country, an undefined area that extended from Lakes Michigan and Superior to the Ohio and Missouri Rivers. French leaders hoped that the Illinois Country, which was governed from distant Canada, would be a rich source of furs and precious metals. Leaders also hoped that a military presence here would pacify the Fox Indians, whose frequent attacks put great pressure on French villages. Though the region failed to yield precious metals, holding the Illinois Country was deemed essential for trade and defense.

Yet surprisingly, the stone Fort de Chartres served as France's Illinois Country headquarters for only ten years. France surrendered Illinois, along with most of its North American possessions, to Great Britain in the 1763 Treaty of Paris that ended the Seven Years' War. British troops of the 42nd Royal Highland Regiment took possession of the fort in 1765. The British made little use of their new possession, which they renamed Fort Cavendish. Erosion by the Mississippi was a continual problem, and in 1771, they abandoned it.

Now an Illinois state park, Fort de Chartres is a reconstruction of the third fort built on this site. The powder magazine was the only original structure still standing when the state of Illinois purchased the site in 1913. The museum contains many artifacts discovered during site excavations.

The annual Rendezvous at Fort de Chartres is held the first full weekend in June to re-create the traditional French fur trapper's holiday of the 18th century. The rendezvous is one of the oldest and largest events of its kind in the nation.

(618) 284-7230 • www.state.il.us/hpa/hs/DeChartres.htm

December 5, 1803

Expedition Entry
Near Crystal City, Missouri
Monday, December 5, 1803

Clark and his men see caves and indented arches in the cliffs on the Missouri side. They pass Platten Creek, with dense settlements of Americans. They dine at a creek with a rock that forms a natural 200-foot-high wharf. On the Illinois side, they come to Eagle Creek, which runs 12 miles from Bellefontaine. They planned to take in provisions here, but when they learn that none have arrived, they proceed a half mile above the landing and camp for the night.

Expedition Entry
Near Arnold, Missouri
Tuesday, December 6, 1803

On this dark, wet morning, Clark learns that Captain Lewis passed through the day before on his way to St. Louis. When the men pass Little Rock Creek, Clark notices several settlements. They also pass the mouth of the Meramec River.

Expedition Entry
Near Cahokia, Illinois
Wednesday, December 7, 1803

The wind becomes so violent on this day that it blows one of the masts off. The men pass a village at the mouth of a large creek, the River Des Peres. This village, called Viele Pauchr (empty pockets, now known as Carondelet), contains a number of French families and is situated about four miles below St. Louis. At 3 p.m. the men come to Cahokia Landing, at the mouth of Cahokia Creek.

Today's Trail
Explore Cahokia, Illinois

Cahokia, the first permanent white settlement in Illinois, was established in 1699 by French Canadian missionaries. Today Cahokia contains some of the few surviving French-colonial buildings still standing in the United States. The most famous is the house at Cahokia Courthouse State Historic Site.

The Cahokia Courthouse is an excellent example of early French log construction known as poteaux-sur-solle (post-on-sill foundation), where the upright hewn logs are seated on a horizontal sill log, with the spaces between filled with stone and mortar chinking.

The courthouse was constructed as a dwelling about 1730, then became a courthouse in 1793, and for twenty years it served as a center of political activity in the Old Northwest Territory. It was visited by Lewis on his way up the Mississippi River. It was later dismantled and reconstructed in St. Louis during the Louisiana Purchase Exposition of 1903.

Be sure to also visit the Nicholas Jarrot Mansion. Captain Lewis met Jarrot, a fur trader on the upper Mississippi, at Kaskaskia in December of 1803. Lewis was accompanied to St. Louis by Jarrot and John Hay, trader and postmaster of Cahokia. Jarrot is mentioned again in Clark's journal on April 2, 1804, when Jarrot passed the Corps' winter camp at Wood River. Jarrot was bound for Prairie du Chien, Wisconsin, to trade.

Jarrot's mansion in Cahokia dates to 1818. The Jarrot House is considered the oldest brick building in Illinois (it was built long before Illinois became a state!).

Cahokia at one time was the seat of government for a huge territory, which included today's 80 northern Illinois counties. However, floods and the growing importance of St. Louis limited Cahokia's grasp on prominence. The county seat moved to Belleville in 1814 and Cahokia reverted to a small agricultural center on the outskirts of East St. Louis.

December 8, 1803

Today's Trail

Explore Cahokia Mounds Historic Site
Collinsville, Illinois

Today, from the top of Monks Mound, you can see across the Mississippi River to downtown St. Louis and the Gateway Arch. This is a fitting location to ponder that when Lewis & Clark embarked on their journey west, they were positioned between the ancient and future civilizations that had come to call this vast territory home. St. Louis had already been bustling with trade for 40 years when Meriwether Lewis arrived late in 1803, but what he perhaps didn't know was that the St. Louis area had been far more populated centuries before—with a population easily as large as the biggest cities of Lewis' time.

At its peak around 1050–1150 A.D., Cahokia was home to between 10,000 and 40,000 Indians. No city in America would be that large for another 800 years. In its day, Cahokia was a major trading center whose ideas and cultural influence extended to cultures throughout much of North America.

Cahokia is the largest prehistoric settlement in North America north of Mexico. Kids who hike to the top of Monks Mound or visit the rebuilt "Woodhenge," will say this place is awesome. Archeologists might use a few more words to say the same thing. They "consider this site a representation of the most complex social and political culture of prehistoric North American Indians."

For more than 1,400 years beginning in 600 B.C., Woodland Indians inhabited the area, developing complex religious, social, economic and political systems. However, it is the building accomplishments that make this site significant. Cahokia was a planned city with elaborate public buildings and residences at the core. Cahokia covered roughly six square miles, only part of which is still visible today, on a low point of land surrounding the confluence of the Missouri, Illinois and Mississippi Rivers.

These industrious people moved an estimated 50 million cubic feet of earth using woven baskets as containers to create a network of mounds. Approximately 100 still exist. As the largest prehistoric earthen construction in the Americas, Monk's

Mound is a testament to the sophisticated engineering skills of these people. Its base covers 14 acres and it rises in four terraces to a height of 100 feet. Atop this would have been a massive building another 50 feet high. There is also a re-created "Woodhenge" of upright logs here, used as a celestial calendar.

For 500 years, Cahokia was the major center of a culture that at its peak stretched from Red Wing, Minnesota, to Key Marco, Florida, and across the Southeast. After about 400 years the population began to decline and the site was abandoned by 1500 A.D. Resource depletion and climate change are possible culprits for the decline. In the late 1600s, the Cahokia Indians came to the area, from which this place received its name.

Expedition Entry
December 8 – 10, 1803

There are no journal entries from these days. The men remain at Cahokia, and Lewis rejoins them after meeting with Spanish Lieutenant Governor Carlos Dehault Delassus, who denies permission to ascend the Missouri River until he gets approval from his superiors. Lewis is not worried, as he knows the party plans to winter at Wood River, and that the territory will be transferred to the United States soon, when the Louisiana Purchase is finalized.

Did you know that a normal tow on the Upper Mississippi consists of 15 barges? Each barge is 195 feet by 35 feet. Each barge holds 1,500 tons. River towboats range in power from 3,000 to 10,500 horsepower. Tows on the middle and lower river can be much larger. The record tow consisted of 72 barges.

December 11, 1803

Expedition Entry
On Gabaret Island, Illinois
Sunday, December 11, 1803

On this rainy morning, the men cross the river to St. Louis. Lewis is detained to acquire information of the country and to prepare dispatches to the government. The men then move on in the rain and eventually camp on the side of a large island on the Illinois side. The current is against the Missouri shore and the banks are falling in.

Expedition Entry
Near Alton, Illinois
Monday, December 12, 1803

The men set out after a night of heavy northwestern winds. On the Missouri side, there is a settlement in a small prairie, perhaps the village of St. Ferdinand, or Florissant. Then they come to the mouth of Wood River. The heavy winds increase to a full-fledged storm with hail and snow. After landing, they see two canoes of Potawatomi Indians land on the opposite bank. Three of the Potawatomi men come across the river in a small canoe. Clark and the Corps' hunters set out on land in different directions and return with turkeys and opossums. The Potawatomi inform him that the country is beautiful and has plenty of game.

*Clark's drawing of the confluence of the Missouri and
Mississippi Rivers, from his journal, circa January 3, 1804.*

Today's Trail

Explore Wood River Museum & Visitors Center
Wood River, Illinois

From November 14 to 19, 1803, Lewis & Clark camped at the junction of the Ohio and Mississippi Rivers. They set sail on the Mississippi River on November 20, and they arrived at the mouth of Wood River in Illinois on December 12, 1803. Here they set up Camp Dubois, their winter headquarters.

The Wood River Museum & Visitors Center, established in 1997, includes a gazebo dedicated to Lewis & Clark. Exhibits in the museum highlight the early days of the town and include a model of the Corps of Discovery's Camp Dubois.

Be sure to also visit the log-hewn replica of Camp Dubois. It is located at the northeast corner of the intersection of Route 143 and Route 3 in Wood River, Illinois. Call to find out more about the rendezvous held here each May, which celebrates the fur trapping era that lasted from 1700 to 1840.

While many towns sprung up in the region during the 19th century, the Wood River valley was largely empty except for railroad tracks and a few scattered farmhouses. The arrival of the Standard Oil Refinery in 1907 changed all that. The main products of the first refinery were kerosene, fuel oil, coke, paraffin and asphalt. By 1911, the company began making gasoline to meet the demand caused by the popularity of the automobile. Workers began to flood into the area to work at the refinery and in 1907, A.E. Benbow, a local entrepreneur, founded Benbow City, a town of saloons, gambling and brothels. The City of Wood River was incorporated in 1908 and developed around Benbow City. Wood River and East Wood River merged in 1911 and annexed Benbow City in 1917.

In the 1920s, Wood River was the one of the fastest growing communities in the country and had more workers than houses. To solve this problem Standard Oil built many Sears catalog homes, which can be seen throughout the community. A concentration of "Honor Built" homes can be found on the east side of the 100 and 200 blocks of 9th Street. South of Wood River is the small town of Roxana, referred to as "The town that

Shell built." Visitors interested in the history of the refineries can visit the Shell History Museum located on Route 111.

(618) 254-1993

www.greatriverroad.com/Cities/Wood/woodMuseum.htm

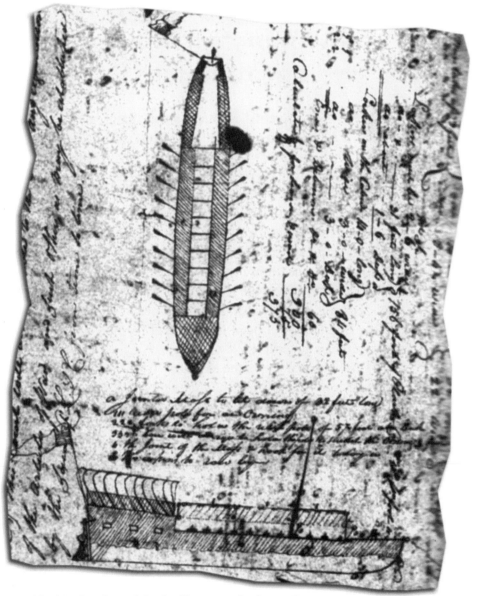

Clark's sketches of the keelboat, made during his stay at Camp Dubois, Wood River, Illinois, circa January 21, 1804.

Region Review

Wood River, Illinois to Washington, Missouri

May 14 – 24, 1804

The Corps of Discovery spent the winter of 1803-04 at a camp the men built called Camp Dubois. It was located at Wood River, Illinois, which was then known as River Dubois. There, William Clark trained his crew for the long, strenuous journey ahead. Meriwether Lewis visited the camp but spent much of the winter at St. Louis, gathering supplies and information for the trek to the Northwest. By the spring of 1804, the transfer of the Louisiana Territory to the United States had been finalized, and Lewis, Clark and their men set out to explore this new American frontier and the mysterious western lands beyond it.

This chapter follows the explorers from their departure from Camp Dubois on the first leg of their journey past the confluence of the Mississippi and Missouri Rivers, heading westward on the Missouri River to their arrival near present-day Washington, Missouri.

Modern-day explorers will enjoy views of the river, historic sites such as the Nathan Boone home, Missouri's scenic wine country and the hospitality of some of the state's memorable rivertowns.

Expedition Entry

Departure from Wood River, Illinois
Near the Confluence of the Missouri & Mississippi Rivers
Monday, May 14, 1804

William Clark and his men leave Camp Dubois at Wood River, Illinois, and row across the Mississippi River to the confluence with the Missouri River, and begin their ascent of the Missouri River. They travel four and a half miles up the Missouri River and camp on an island near Coldwater Creek. Lewis remains in St. Louis to take care of last-minute affairs and eventually joins Clark at St. Charles, Missouri.

There has been some debate over the Corps of Discovery's official departure point. Some people think of St. Louis as the explorers' Gateway to the West, while others assert that the journey officially began when Lewis joined Clark at St. Charles and they set out together with their Corps of Discovery.

In his journal, Lewis writes: "The mouth of the River Dubois is to be considered as the point of departure."

Today's Trail

Explore the Confluence Monument & the Illinois Lewis & Clark State Historic Site Hartford, Illinois

This 14,000-square-foot exhibition offers numerous displays and multimedia presentations on the Lewis & Clark expedition, including a cutaway keelboat—a full-size replica of the 55-foot Corps of Discovery's vessel. This boat is open on one side to reveal hidden interior passages, storage compartments, living quarters and cargo. Explore the replica of the winter quarters of Camp Dubois, as well as a 150-foot-high Lewis & Clark Memorial Tower, which offers a panoramic view of the confluence of the Mississippi and Missouri Rivers.

(618) 251-5811 • www.campdubois.com

Opposite page: The Missouri & Mississippi Rivers confluence offers hiking and bird watching opportunities at many conservation areas and state parks.

Today's Trail
Explore the Confluence of the Missouri & Mississippi Rivers
St. Louis Riverfront, Missouri

Clark and his men paddled through the confluence of the Mississippi and Missouri Rivers on May 14, 1804, as they left their winter camp at Camp Dubois in Wood River, Illinois, and began their ascent of the Mighty Mo.

Great places to enjoy this stretch of river are the Columbia Bottoms Conservation Area, the Ted & Pat Jones–Confluence Point State Park, Old Chain of Rocks Bridge, the St. Louis Riverfront Trail and the Riverfront Heritage Trail Connection, all part of a comprehensive Confluence Greenway project, which when completed, will be a 40-mile-long riverside recreation and conservation area on both banks of the Mississippi extending from the Gateway Arch to the Mississippi's confluence with the Missouri and Illinois Rivers.

As part of the larger St. Louis 2004 project celebrating the Lewis & Clark Bicentennial and the 1904 St. Louis World's Fair, the Confluence Greenway creates a popular one-of-a-kind destination for countless visitors. Its parks and trails offer unprecedented access to the waterfront for hiking, biking, fishing, bird watching, river watching and much more.

(314) 436-1324 • www.confluencegreenway.org

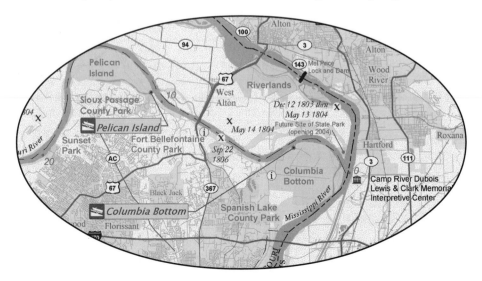

Peering up at the St. Louis Arch from its base gives you a whole new perspective. Explore the Museum of Westward Expansion located directly below the arch. Take the "egg" tram to the top of the arch, watch a large-screen movie, peruse their gift shop (stocked with Lewis & Clark booty) and enjoy their extensive Lewis & Clark–themed exhibits.

Today's Trail
Explore St. Louis, Missouri

The small village of St. Louis in Lewis' lifetime was home to only about 1,000 people. The inhabitants were mainly French-Canadian trappers who made the city the center of fur trade for the huge region drained by the Missouri River. Popular trail stops along today's trail are highlighted on the next few pages. Call the St. Louis Convention and Visitors Commission for a complete lowdown on Lewis & Clark related events.

(800) 916-8938 • (800) 325-7962 • www.explorestlouis.com

Today's Trail
Explore the Museum of Westward Expansion
St. Louis, Missouri

Located beneath the Gateway Arch, the Museum of Westward Expansion displays the history of America's westward movement. Murals depict scenes from along Lewis & Clark's route with descriptions from their journals. Life-sized animatronic figures of Lewis, Clark and American Indians bring the story to life. Also housed here is the world's largest collection of American Indian Peace Medals.

Jefferson National Expansion Memorial consists of the Gateway Arch, the Museum of Westward Expansion and the Old St. Louis Courthouse. The Museum of Westward Expansion, located below the Arch, is as large as a football field and contains an extensive collection of artifacts, mounted animal specimens, a teepee and an overview of the expedition.

Prominent figures in America's pioneering history come to life through animated audio presentations. Thomas Jefferson talks about his many accomplishments, William Clark speaks of his western expedition, a Buffalo Soldier recounts his struggles after the Civil War and an 1846 woman headed west tells her story.

During a nationwide competition in 1948, architect Eero Saarinen's inspired design for a 630-foot stainless steel arch was chosen as a perfect monument to the spirit of the western pioneers. Construction of the arch began in 1963 and was completed in October of 1965, for a total cost of less than $15 million. The arch has foundations sunk 60 feet into the ground, and is built to withstand earthquakes and high winds. It is built to sway up to 18 inches. Save time by purchasing tram and movie tickets in advance online at www.stlouisarch.com.

(877) 982-1410 • www.nps.gov/jeff

Today's Trail

Explore St. Louis' Old Courthouse

Located just two blocks west of the Arch, the Old Courthouse is one of the oldest standing buildings in St. Louis (construction began in 1839). It was here that the first two trials of the Dred Scott case were held in 1847 and 1850. Today, the building houses restored courtrooms and a museum charting the

---

Did you know that the Arch and the Jefferson National Expansion Memorial rest on the site of William Clark's house?

Did you know the Drury Plaza at 2 S. 4th Street is housed in the former American Fur Exchange? The bronze diorama of Lewis & Clark in their lobby is top notch. (314) 231-3003.

---

history of the city of St. Louis. Here you can view a film that depicts the role of St. Louis in the history of the United States, as well as see a diorama portraying the transfer of the Upper Louisiana Territory, which both Lewis and Clark attended.

Missouri artist Gary Lucy will host an exhibit here *Inland Waterways: The Highways of Our Heritage,* from September 3, 2004 through January 8, 2005. Lucy will be exhibiting the culmination of more than two decades painting life along the Missouri River, including the steamboat era and Lewis and Clark. Located at 11 North Fourth Street.

(314) 655-1600 • www.nps.gov/jeff

Today's Trail

Explore St. Louis' Laclede's Landing

Walk the ancient cobblestones of St. Louis' riverfront district. Enjoy great outdoor dining at Hannegans Restaurant, shown below, as well as many other restaurants. Laclede's Landing is also home to many bars with live music and a second-rate wax museum. The Landing has parking for the nearby casino and other area attractions.

Hannegan's Restaurant and several others at Laclede's Landing offer outdoor dining within walking distance of the Arch.

THOMAS JEFFERSON

The Jefferson Memorial site at the Missouri History Museum was the main entrance to the 1904 World's Fair.

Missouri History Museum Curator Carolyn Gilman is author of the book Lewis and Clark: Across the Divide, *a companion book to the national bicentennial exhibit.*

Today's Trail

Explore the Missouri History Museum
Forest Park, St. Louis, Missouri

The Missouri History Museum at Forest Park in St. Louis is another must-visit site for Lewis & Clark enthusiasts. Visit the re-creation of William Clark's council room. Clark's journal, his clothing and other artifacts of the expedition are part of an extensive Lewis & Clark collection at the museum. For the general museum, admission is free on Tuesdays from 4 to 8 p.m.

(314) 746-4599 • www.mohistory.org

Rare items from the expedition, such as Clark's elk-hide journal, will be exhibited together in one place.

In 2004, the museum is hosting a major exhibition mounted by the Missouri Historical Society to commemorate the voyage. The 6,000-square-foot exhibition will be a reunion of hundreds of artifacts and documents that have not been seen in one place since 1806. Interestingly enough, many expedition items were auctioned off as army surplus, netting the government $408. This exhibit will display the culmination of five years spent tracking down these rare items. One item was spotted on *Antique Road Show*. Others cropped up in the hands of a traveling circus troupe.

The exhibit *Lewis & Clark: The National Bicentennial Exhibition* will be in St. Louis through September of 2004. It will then embark on a coast-to-coast tour with stops from coast to coast. Call to check on exhibit admission prices: (314) 454-3150 or go online to www.lewisandclarkexhibit.org.

The year 2004 is also the centennial of the 1904 World's Fair held in St. Louis. There will be an opening weekend Centennial Celebration held at Forest Park April 30 – May 2, 2004. This three-day extravaganza will take place around the Grand Basin in Forest Park at the foot of Art Hill. The weekend kicks off with an opening ceremony modeled on the one that took place in 1904, call (314) 426-7519.

Today's Trail

Explore Bellefontaine Cemetery
St. Louis, Missouri

Here, a tall granite obelisk and a bronze bust of the explorer mark William Clark's final resting place. Above the grave site, a plaque reads, "Soldier, Explorer, Statesman and Patriot. His Life is Written in the History of His Country." According to Mike Tiemann, the cemetery superintendent, Clark's grave site, located in the northeast corner of the grounds, is the most visited monument in the cemetery.

Stop by the gray stone office just inside the main gate to pick up a free tour map of the cemetery's 300 acres and 14 miles of roads, all in a park-like setting.

"The current visitor's guide only gives the locations of 40 famous graves, but Bellefontaine contains at least 500 graves of extreme historical significance," Mike said.

Open daily until 5 p.m. The office closes at 4 p.m. Located at 4947 West Florissant Avenue. (314) 381-0750.

Be sure to visit the Nez Perce Warriors Monument at nearby Calvary Cemetery. The site is marked by two eight-foot-tall granite eagle feathers with a narrative about how in 1831, four Nez Perce warriors arrived in St. Louis to visit with Clark, whom they had met during his expedition. Two of the warriors died shortly after arriving in St. Louis after being exposed to new ailments and lacking immunity, and they were interred here.

Today's Trail
Explore Fort Belle Fontaine Park
St. Louis, Missouri

Established in 1805 on the south, low-lying bank of the Missouri River, near the confluence of the Mississippi River, Belle Fontaine was the first U.S. military post located in the newly acquired Louisiana Territory. The Corps of Discovery spent the final night of their expedition here on September 22, 1806, before heading downriver to St. Louis.

Belle Fontaine served as an American Indian "factory" or trading post for local Sac, Fox and other American Indian tribes. General James Wilkinson, first governor of the Louisiana Territory and military commander, selected the site. The factory was removed from Fort Belle Fontaine in 1808, with part of the trade goods sent to Fort Osage on the Missouri River (near Kansas City). Read more about Fort Osage on page 174.

From its early days, the Belle Fontaine site served as the launching or stopover point for a number of expeditions to the far reaches of the American West. Among those explorers was pioneering military officer Zebulon Pike. His trips up the Mississippi in 1805 and along the Missouri River in 1806 both left from here, as well as the 1818 Yellowstone Expedition and the scientific expedition of Stephen Long. In 1826, Fort Belle Fontaine was abandoned by the U.S. Army and replaced by Jefferson Barracks (1826 – 1946) in southern St. Louis County.

On the Corps' return trip to St. Louis on September 22, 1806, John Ordway wrote, "towards evening we arived at Bell fountain a Fort or cantonement on South Side which was built since we ascended the Missourie & a handsome place... the Company of Artillery who lay at this fort fired 17 Rounds with the field peaces."

Also of note, in his years as governor of the Louisiana Territory, Meriwether Lewis made frequent trips via horseback from St. Louis over "Bellefontaine Road" to socialize with old Army friends at Fort Belle Fontaine.

While on the grounds, be sure to visit the grand stone staircase with sweeping views of the Missouri River. It was built by the Works Progress Administration (WPA) in 1936. You can hike one- to three-mile trails through the area.

Several informative signs describe Lewis & Clark's activities in and around Fort Belle Fontaine. The original Lewis & Clark campsites are now underwater as the Missouri River channel has shifted over time. You can also see the spring that inspired the fort's name, which is sometimes visible from the trail, depending on the height of the river. There is also a period cannon here, and the site of a saw and gristmill built in the 1700s on what was part of an 850-acre Spanish land grant.

Each September, there is an encampment and black powder shoot. In October, a historic hayride tour is offered, where visitors can talk with reenactors at their campfires and listen to their stories.

(314) 544-5714

www.stlouisco.com/parks/ftbellefontaine.html

Dip one toe in the Missouri River and one in the Mississippi at the Edward "Ted" and Pat Jones–Confluence Point State Park, located at the confluence of our country's two great rivers: (636) 940-3325.

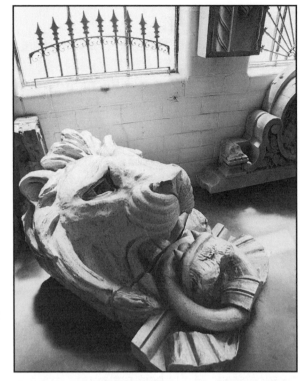

Opposite page: The stuff of my mother's nightmares: me (with a huge smile) climbing a safe but quasi-precarious walkway to a gutted airplane hull suspended high above by guy wires.

See epic pieces of early salvaged architecture at the City Museum. They don't build them like that anymore!

Today's Trail

Explore the St. Louis City Museum

Let's face it—the theme of your Lewis & Clark trip is "explore more." Well, there's no better place to let the kids do just that. This place is a child's dream come true. You get to touch, climb, crawl, stomp, dangle, swing, bounce, squeeze, smoosh and more! From a kid's perspective, this is how the world is supposed to be—from crawling up a whale's soft tongue to climbing through an eagle's nest. There's fun here for kids of all ages. The whir of the ancient shoelace machine is entrancing. Watch potters pot or belt out a song like Bob Dylan in the Beat Cafe. The only thing you can't do here is get bored. Call for discount rate times and special events. Located downtown at 701 North 15th Street.

(314) 231-CITY • www.citymuseum.org

Today's Trail

Explore Columbia Bottom Conservation Area
St. Louis, Missouri

This 4,318-acre area offers a front-row seat to view the confluence of the Missouri and Mississippi Rivers, as well as ongoing conservation efforts. Recreational opportunities abound. While in the area, be sure to also visit the new Ted and Pat Jones–Confluence State Park, which offers great Lewis & Clark interpretation and river views. Call the Department of Natural Resources for more information: (800) 334-6946.

(636) 441-4554 • www.conservation.state.mo.us

Today's Trail

Explore Pelican Island Natural Area
St. Louis, Missouri

This 2,260-acre area, located on the Missouri River in northern St. Louis County, is accessible only to boaters. The site preserves one of the best remaining examples of what the islands on the lower Missouri River looked like before the river was channelized. It features a bottomland forest, shifting sandbars and mudflats.

(636) 441-4554 • www.conservation.state.mo.us

Expedition Entry

Near Black Walnut, Missouri
Tuesday, May 15, 1804

After traveling nine and a half miles, the men camp on the north shore at Piper's Landing. A heavily laden stern causes the keelboat to become stuck on logs in the water three times. Clark notes that one of the pirogues is undermanned and its crew has trouble keeping up. He writes of passing a site called the Plattes, where he sees a flat rock projecting from the foot of a hill.

Today's Trail

Explore St. Stanislaus Conservation Area
St. Louis, Missouri

This 810-acre area is named for the St. Stanislaus Seminary, which was once located here. For a view of the Missouri River bottom, visitors can hike to a bluff that early French explorers named La Charbonier, or coal seam. Clark makes note of the area's coal resources when they pass by.

(636) 441-4554 • www.conservation.state.mo.us

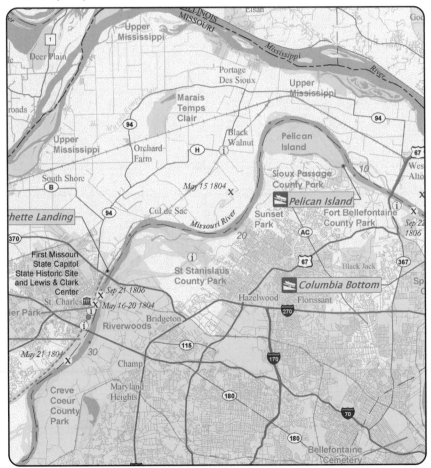

Clark and his men rowed through the confluence of the Mississippi and Missouri Rivers on May 14, 1804, as they left their winter camp at Camp Dubois in Wood River, Illinois, and began their ascent of the Mighty Mo. They arrived in St. Charles on May 16, 1804.

*Frontier Park in St. Charles has a large bronze sculpture of Lewis
& Clark, along with Lewis' trusty Newfoundland dog, Seaman.*

Expedition Entry

St. Charles, Missouri
Wednesday, May 16 – Monday, May 21, 1804

Clark arrives on May 16 with the keelboat, two pirogues and about 40 men. He notes that the village of St. Charles is about one mile in length and consists of about 450 people who are primarily French. The village was founded as Les Petites Cotes, which means 'the little hills,' and the Spanish knew it as San Carlos del Misuri. While waiting for Lewis to arrive from St. Louis, the men make final purchases and enjoy the hospitality of the inhabitants. Residents invite the men to dinners and a dance, and they also attend a church service. This will be their last visit to an established town for about two and a half years.

On May 17, three members of the Corps of Discovery are court martialed for being absent without leave. One of them, John Collins, is also charged with behaving in an unbecoming manner at a ball and using disrespectful language. Collins is found guilty and sentenced to "fifty lashes on his naked back." The other men, William Warner and Hugh Hall, are granted leniency. Lewis arrives in St. Charles on May 20 with some well-wishers from St. Louis.

The next day, Clark writes, "Set out from St. Charles at three oClock after getting every matter arranged, proceeded on under a jentle Breese."

Foul weather just a mile upriver prevents them from traveling more than four miles, so they set up camp on the first island. It rains "powerfully" throughout the night.

*St. Charles' Main Street, Missouri's largest historic district,
is just a block away from the Katy Trail. Take your time and explore.*

*Let a carriage ride take you back to the sights and
sounds of St. Charles' bustling riverport past.*

Today's Trail
Explore St. Charles, Missouri

Main Street in St. Charles is the largest historic district in
Missouri. It includes 125 craft and specialty shops. Visitors can
explore the restored Missouri's first state capitol. Walk to the
Missouri River's edge at Frontier Park and see where the Corps of
Discovery set out on May 21, 1804, under a gentle breeze. The
annual Lewis & Clark Heritage Days are held the third weekend of
May to commemorate this event. Don't miss it.

St. Charles is also the site where, on May 17, 1804, three
members of the Corps of Discovery were court martialed for
being absent without leave (see page 87).

St. Charles is also where Francois Labiche, a half-Indian,
half-Frenchman, and Pierre Cruzatte joined the expedition. Just
before departure, Pierre Chouteau assisted in recruiting other
"engagés," skilled French boatmen who would escort the Corps
to Fort Mandan in present-day North Dakota.

St. Charles will host a Lewis & Clark Bicentennial National Signature Event May 14 – 23, 2004. Call the Greater St. Charles Convention & Visitors Bureau for a complete listing of Lewis & Clark related events planned for 2004 and beyond.

The Lewis & Clark Boathouse and Nature Center features exhibits on the expedition, and you can view replicas of the explorers' keelboat and two pirogues, when they are not out on reenactments or away at events.

Annual river clean ups offer you a direct way to get involved with the river. Volunteer for a clean up on the Missouri or Mississippi Rivers: www.riverrelief.org. These efforts are coordinated by Missouri River Relief, in conjunction with Chad Pregracke and Living Lands and Waters. Over the past decade, Chad, his full-time staff, and thousands of community volunteers have cleaned up stretches of the Mississippi, Ohio and Missouri Rivers.

Be sure to visit the nearby Weldon Spring Conservation Area for pristine views of the river easily accessible by car. Or hike the Weldon Spring Hollow Natural Area, the site of a pristine Missouri forest, and home to many native plants.

Boone's Lick Trail Inn Bed & Breakfast is located in the heart of historic St. Charles, within easy walking distance of many historic sites, the riverfront park, the casino, shops and restaurants.

*Don't miss the Lewis
& Clark Heritage
Days held the third
weekend of May.*

Call the Greater
St. Charles Convention
& Visitors Bureau for
a complete listing of
Lewis & Clark related
activities, sites and
area lodging options.
(800) 366-2427
www.historicstcharles.com

Harry Winland unfurls the U.S. flag during a Lewis & Clark reenactment. His military dress is what the military crewmembers would have worn during the early stages of the expedition. Opposite page top: Reenactors from throughout the country have come together to help put a face on history. Opposite page bottom: Crewmember C.J. Lanahan, portraying Sergeant Ordway, tells his story to an attentive future crew member.

Join the Discovery Expedition of St. Charles

*H*undreds of volunteers from across the country have joined forces to reenact Lewis & Clark's epic journey. The Discovery Expedition of St. Charles has traveled thousands of miles on the rivers of Lewis & Clark, in replicas of the keelboat and two pirogues used by the expedition on the lower Missouri River. The group was designated as official reenactors for the National Lewis & Clark Bicentennial. As official reenactors, they are retracing the entire waterway portion of the original 1803 – 1806 expedition east of the Rockies.

The Lewis & Clark Boat House and Nature Center in St. Charles, shown above, is a must visit. Be sure to visit the Trading Post and meet Mimi and Darold Jackson, at left, who operate the center and have been very active in Lewis & Clark education for many years.

Schedule your trip to coincide with one of their river stops. Or visit the crew's website to read modern-day journal entries and to learn about their educational outreach program, which allows students to interact with crew members through videoconferencing. Their schedule of river stops is online at http://lewisandclark.net. Support this organization by joining. With your membership, you will receive a newsletter and be able to learn more about taking part in future reenactments.

While traveling the Lewis & Clark Trail in St. Charles, be sure to stop at the Discovery Expedition's headquarters, the

Lewis & Clark Boat House and Nature Center. This is where the boats are housed when they are not on the river. In addition to learning more about the reenactment, the museum features exhibits relating to the Lewis and Clark expedition and the Missouri River ecosystem. Their gift shop has an excellent array of goodies for trail trekkers. The Boat House is located on the riverfront, near Frontier Park, at Bishop's Landing. The landing is near the casino at 1050 Riverside Drive. Open Monday through Saturday 10 a.m. – 5 p.m. and Sunday noon to 5 p.m.
(636) 947-3199 • http://lewisandclark.net

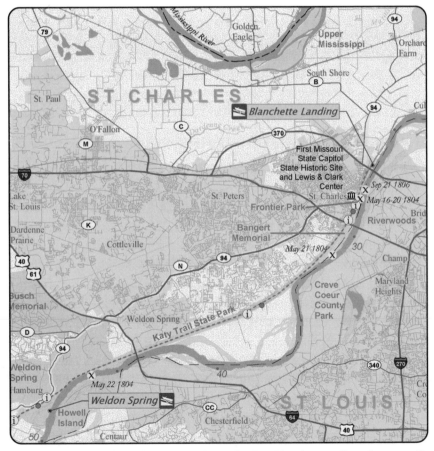

If you pedal the Katy Trail west from the St. Charles trailhead, you will arrive in the scenic Weldon Spring Conservation Area in 16.5 miles.

The Katy Trail passes through several large culverts as it winds its way west from St. Charles, which is the easternmost trailhead.

Today's Trail
Explore the Katy Trail State Park
St. Charles, Missouri

Much of Lewis & Clark's journey across Missouri can be followed by traveling on the Katy Trail, a former railroad right-of-way that was converted into a 225-mile bike path, making it America's longest rails-to-trails project. St. Charles is the easternmost trailhead. The trail winds along the Missouri River valley from St. Charles heading west to Boonville, 152 miles later, and then veers away from the river and heads southwest through woodlands, farmland and prairie to Clinton, Missouri. It passes through historic rivertowns that feature local wineries, bed & breakfasts, and campgrounds. The trail's flat gravel surface makes it easy to follow in Lewis & Clark's footsteps, and bikes can be rented along the way. The trail is highlighted in its entirety along with detailed camping, hotel and bed & breakfast information in *The Complete Katy Trail Guidebook*.

(800) 334-6946 • www.katytrailstatepark.com

Today's Trail

Explore the August A. Busch Memorial Conservation Area
Near St. Charles, Missouri

This 6,900-acre area is a great spot for bird watching, hiking and fishing on the area's 32 small lakes. Visitors can also enjoy an eight-mile driving tour of the area. 2360 Highway D.
(636) 441-4554 • www.conservation.state.mo.us

Today's Trail

Explore Weldon Spring Conservation Area
Weldon Spring, Missouri

This 7,300-acre site offers hiking, mountain biking trails and roads that lead to the Missouri River for scenic views. If you are pedaling the Katy Trail west from the St. Charles trailhead, you will arrive in this scenic area in 16.5 miles.
(636) 441-4554 • www.conservation.state.mo.us

Expedition Entry

Near Weldon Spring, Missouri
Tuesday, May 22, 1804

The Corps of Discovery sets out on this cloudy morning and passes several small farms, Bonhomme Creek and a camp of Kickapoo Indians. The men camp at a bend in the river and the Kickapoo arrive to give the crew a gift of four deer. The men offer two quarts of whiskey in exchange.

Today's Trail

Explore Labadie & St. Albans, Missouri

St. Albans is a small community near where Lewis almost fell off a tall bluff, stopping his tumbling descent with his knife (see May 23, 1804 journal entry). An interpretive sign tells the tale. A French restaurant here makes for a nice stop. Explore nearby Labadie, which has great shops and fine dining.

Expedition Entry
Near St. Albans, Missouri
Wednesday, May 23, 1804

After running into a log, the men are delayed for an hour. They then pass Femme Osage Creek, where there is an American settlement of 30 or 40 families. Daniel Boone established the community in 1799.

After leaving the keelboat and crew to get a better view of nearby Tavern Cave, a popular stop for river travelers of the day, Lewis scrambles up the bluff to survey the country ahead. Lewis tumbles down a steep bluff face 300 feet above the river. As the loose rock breaks way underfoot and Lewis falls towards his imminent death, he drives his knife into the crumbling rock and soil to arrest his fall.

Clark writes: "we passed a large Cave. … (called by the french the Tavern) — about 120 feet wide 40 feet Deep & 20 feet high. many different immages are Painted on the Rock at this place. The Inds. and French pay omage. Many names are wrote on the rock, Stoped about one mile above for Capt Lewis who had assended the Clifts... hanging over the Water... Capt. Lewis near falling from the... rocks 300 feet, he caught at 20 foot."

The painting on the opposite page, *Meriwether Lewis Escapes Death Above Tavern Cave* by Missouri artist Michael Haynes, captures Lewis' precarious fall noted in Clark's journal entry above.

Michael's Lewis & Clark inspired panoramic vision of the Missouri River valley in 1804 can be seen at the Discovery Center on the Kansas City Plaza (see page 188). Michael is also the co-author of *Lewis & Clark: Tailor Made, Trail Worn: Army Life, Clothing & Weapons of the Corps of Discovery.* Visit his website to view more expedition artwork: www.mhaynesart.com.

Today's Trail

Explore the Shaw Nature Reserve
Gray Summit, Missouri

Explore the enchanted forest to find the woodland gazebo, walk through a tapestry of color in the eight-acre wildflower garden, go bird watching among the picturesque log cabins and enjoy the day hiking on the reserve's extensive network of trails through forests, tallgrass prairies, riverbottoms and wetlands.

Located southwest of St. Louis at the intersection of Highways 44 and 100, the 2,500-acre reserve is the perfect place to hike and imagine how Missouri must have looked in its earlier, more pristine state. A scenic driving tour offers a dazzling daffodil display in the spring.

Start at the stone visitors center (there is a small entrance fee), where the helpful staff offer an area overview and a map. Ask about the reserve's guided walks, browse the bookstore and peruse the garden shop. Visit the Bascom House, built in 1879, which displays Native American artifacts found onsite as well as interesting environmental and conservation exhibits. During the annual Prairie Days event, period artisans, tipis, reenactors and music bring early settlement days to life.

(636) 451-3512 • www.mobot.org/MOBOT/naturereserve/

Today's Trail
Explore the Nathan Boone Home & Boonesfield Village
Defiance, Missouri

Daniel Boone spent his last living days on this site, at this picturesque four-story home built in the early 1800s (shown above). Also located on the grounds is Boonesfield Village, a replica of an early community. Structures in the village reflect the era of the Louisiana Purchase and the early days of Missouri's statehood, offering a living-history experience throughout the year. Located at 1868 Highway F.

(636) 798-2005

Today's Trail
Explore Augusta, Missouri

Located in the heart of Missouri's Weinstrasse, or wine road, this quaint rivertown is known for being picture perfect. It is a popular getaway for St. Louisans, who flock here to enjoy the wineries, the tasteful antique shops and its many B&Bs.

(636) 228-4005 • www.augusta-missouri.com

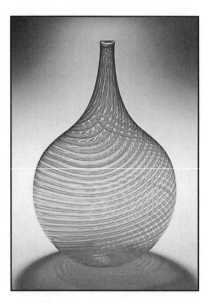

Dancing Light at Sam Stang's Augusta Glass

*T*he picturesque streets of Augusta are lined with bed & breakfasts, antique shops, little cafes and several craft studios, including Sam Stang's Augusta Glass. The vibrant hues of blue on the building's "Goodyear" storefront act as a colorful exclamation point that seems to say that this old building's heyday is now.

The front windows of this now defunct gas station were once lined with oil and fan belts but now they display a gallery of glass that will take your breath away. Sunlight dances through neon oranges, aqua marines, pure yellows, deep reds and gentle greens in a maze of perfectly intersecting lines like something out of a frenetically paced Spiro-graph.

I have yet to find a banana or apple worthy of his fruit bowls. Sam's bowls and drinking vessels are all about high art (and perhaps functionality), but to me, they seem better suited to be on display with gallery lighting. The geometry of his work is too spellbinding to cover up.

Sam Stang does strong and intricate work, with clear evidence of its roots in the Italian tradition of glassblowing. His work is available in many fine galleries throughout the country as well as at his studio gallery in Augusta, Missouri. Other locations to purchase his glass along the Lewis & Clark Trail in

Missouri include the Craft Alliance and the St. Louis Art Museum Shop in St. Louis and at Bluestem Missouri Crafts in Columbia.

"All of my pieces are made by using traditional European glassblowing techniques," Sam said. "With the *murrini* pieces, I begin by making glass rods which are patterned in cross section. The rods are cooled and cut into thin pieces and arranged on an iron plate which is then heated to fuse the *murrini*. This is then rolled into a tube on the end of a blowpipe and shaped into the final form."

"Every piece I make is entirely produced hot at the furnace. The banded bowls are blown as separate sections and fused together. This technique, known as *incalmo,* requires a great deal of skill and cooperation. I work with at least one assistant and often with a team of three experienced glassblowers. For the last four years, Kaeko Maehata has been my main assistant."

Sam Stang attended Washington University in St. Louis and was a student of Fritz Dreisbach at Penland School of Crafts. He was also a student of Lino Tagliapietra at Haystack Mountain School of Crafts in Maine. Sam was a founding partner in Ibex Glass Studio and started Augusta Glass Studio in 1992.

When in Augusta, please keep in mind this is a working studio—don't be surprised to find the gallery closed to visitors on glassblowing days. And don't take it personally—many of Sam's pieces take weeks of concentrated effort. It's not something he can just put down while he gabs with folks coming in to look around. With that said, just peeking in the front window and watching the light dance off of his creations will make the stop worthwhile. Visit his website for some wonderful "eye candy."

(636) 228-4732
www.samstang.com

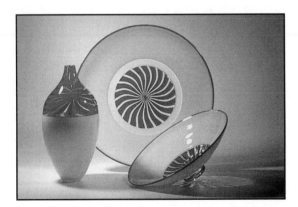

May 24, 1804

Expedition Entry
Near Washington, Missouri
Thursday, May 24, 1804

The crew passes half a mile of projecting rocks called the Devil's race ground (known today as Liffecue Rocks). Their progress is delayed when a strong current catches the keelboat as it passes a sandbar. The current is so strong, it breaks the tow rope and causes the boat to turn end-to-end three times before it finally comes to rest in deep water. In his journal, Clark writes, "this place being the worst I ever Saw, I call it the retregrade bend." As you will soon read, Clark was to revise his "worst I ever saw" many times in the weeks ahead. Despite these troubles, the boats travel ten miles upriver today.

Today's Trail
Explore Washington, Missouri

Washington traces its roots back to the early 1820s, when it served as a ferry landing and later as a steamboat landing on the Missouri River. The area was settled by followers of Daniel Boone and early German immigrants. In 1855, John Busch, the older brother of Adolphus Busch, started a brewery here that bottled the original Busch Beer. The area has numerous wineries, a wonderful riverfront with boat ramp, a historic downtown full of shops, a centrally located Amtrak train stop, and the only factory in the world that still manufactures corncob pipes. The annual Washington Art Fair & Wine Fest in May is not to be missed. Call (636) 239-1743.

Be sure to visit the Gary R. Lucy Gallery, at 231 West Main Street, which features many of artist Gary Lucy's paintings that were inspired by the Lewis & Clark expedition. I have explored many parts of the Missouri River with Gary, and I was always impressed by how he is able to capture the spirit of the river in his incredibly detailed paintings.

Original paintings, prints, postcards, notecards and even puzzles of his works are available at this kid-friendly gallery. You will be amazed at his life-like paintings of early riverboat travel, his collection of riverboat models and his stunning wildlife paintings that have won countless awards. Check out his website to read his river journals, see his artwork and let his images take you back to the rivers of yesterday.

View Lucy's exhibit *Inland Waterways: The Highways of Our Heritage* from September 3, 2004 through January 8, 2005, at the Old Courthouse in St. Louis. This exhibit will contain more than 100 original Lucy paintings completed over a 20-year time period. The works will tell the story of the rivers of America and the role they played in the building of America. Visit www.garylucy.com or call (636) 239-6337.

At the Washington Visitors Center, ask about touring nearby La Charette Village & Fur Trading Post. Located on a Missouri River bluff, this reconstruction of La Charette has a 1790 – 1815 trading post, village houses and period furnishings. The host and guide, Wheelock Crosby Brown, is the former chief of Missouri state historic and archaeological sites.

(888) 792-7466 • www.washmo.org

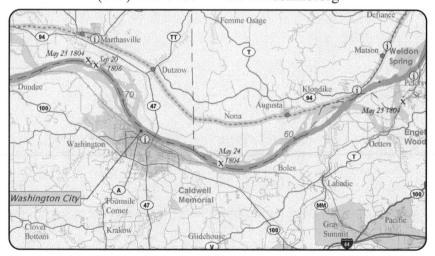

After departing St. Charles on May 20, 1804, the Corps of Discovery traveled up the Missouri River for five days before landing at La Charette, the western-most permanent settlement of French-Canadians they were to encounter, near present-day Marthasville.

Region Review

Marthasville to Rocheport, Missouri

May 25 – June 6, 1804

D uring the late spring of 1804, the Corps of Discovery passed La Charette, the farthest west white settlement on the Missouri River, and the men entered lands that had, until their arrival, been known only to American Indians, fur traders and a few earlier explorers.

The days on the river became warmer and longer, and the voyagers endured heavy rains as they made their way to the central part of Missouri. During this time, both Meriwether Lewis and William Clark collected measurements and observations of the land, flora and fauna around them, and their boats made steady progress on the river.

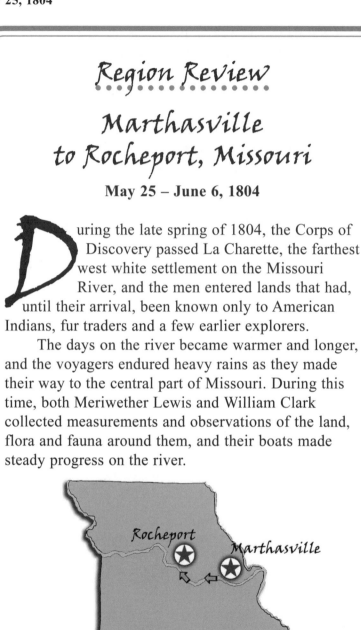

Expedition Entry
Near Marthasville, Missouri
Friday, May 25, 1804

After spending another rainy night on the Missouri River, the Corps of Discovery travels ten miles today, passing several small creeks and an island and then camping at the mouth of a creek near a small French village called La Charette. There are seven families living here in what would be the westernmost settlement of French Canadians that the Corps of Discovery would encounter. The families settled this remote area to more easily hunt the area's abundant game and to trade with the local Native American tribes. Clark writes "The people at this Village is pore, houses Small, they Sent us milk & eggs to eat."

Today's Trail
Explore Marthasville, Missouri

Today Marthasville is a Katy Trail biker's oasis. A popular bike shop, Scenic Cycles, several cafes and bed and breakfasts offer modern-day explorers a respite that Lewis & Clark would surely have enjoyed.

Daniel Boone's arrival in 1799 signaled that American colonization was reaching further westward. After the Louisiana Purchase in 1803, French settlers started selling their claims around the tiny hamlet of La Charette (noted in Clark's journals above) to Americans. La Charette is remembered as the last white settlement the expedition was to encounter on their trip up the Missouri River. The French settlement became an American one when Dr. John Young founded Marthasville nearby on higher ground, named after his wife Martha.

(636) 433-5242 • www.marthasville.org
(636) 433-2909 • www.scenic-cycles.com

Today's Trail

Explore New Haven, Missouri

New Haven is a picture-perfect rivertown worth exploring. Visitors will find food, lodging and a nice vantage point to photograph the Missouri River. Browse the area's great little shops and enjoy the numerous places to eat.

Be sure to visit Robller's Winery, located near the water tower, at 275 Robller Vineyard Road. The winery is a relaxing place to uncork a bottle of Missouri wine and enjoy the afternoon breeze. The wide open lawns near the vineyards are a perfect place to let the kids fly a kite. This family-owned winery, run by the Mueller family and their friendly staff, demonstrate how hospitality, having fun and working hard are at the root of many of the small businesses that make traveling the Lewis & Clark Trail in Missouri so rewarding.

Robller's annual winemaker's dinner is a top-notch event sure to impress your girlfriend or wife. Their "Jammin' in the Vineyard" music series offers some great outdoor fun. Check out their website for more information, www.robllerwines.com, or call (573) 237-3986.

Read the excellent book *Courageous Colter and Companions* by the late New Haven author Lillian Ruth Colter-Frick, the great-great-great-granddaughter of John Colter, member of the Corps of Discovery. The book details Colter's amazing, adventure-filled life and the men of his time, including the expedition's captains, Manuel Lisa, Frederick Bates, Nathan Boone, Thomas James, the Chouteau family and other companions of Colter. Look for the book in Washington and New Haven, or order this 660-page book (79 of those pages are index), directly from Pebble Publishing, Inc. at (573) 698-3903.

Opposite page: New Haven is like something out of a Norman Rockwell painting. Park your car and stroll. See where your feet take you.

Names To Know
John Colter

olter was Lewis & Clark's Mr. Fix-It, the trusted assistant summoned to solve troublesome problems. Colter originally joined the expedition as one of the "nine young men from Kentucky." As the expedition was returning home, Colter received permission to join two fur traders heading back up along the Missouri River and into the Northern Rockies. There he remained for six years.

He was also probably the first explorer to visit Yellowstone, referred to at the time as Colter's Hell. He was also known for his legendary Colter's Run—his daring escape from the pursuit of Blackfeet Indians. Colter later married and settled near Dundee, Missouri, where he died around 1813. Historians continue to debate which of several nearby country cemeteries he is buried in. He left behind many descendants in the New Haven area.

Expedition Entry
Near Berger Bend Conservation Area
Saturday, May 26, 1804

Today the Corps sets out at 7 a.m. after a heavy shower. A stiff wind allows them to "proceed on verry well under sale," which was not a common occurrence for them on the Lower Missouri.

"George Drewyer and John Shields, Sent by Land with the two horses with directions to proceed on one day and hunt the next," Clark writes. They camp that night on an island below Loutre Island (otter in French).

Lewis and Clark lay out orders for the detachment of the crew and their organization. Three squads are formed under Sergeants Floyd, Ordway and Pryor, totaling 26 men. This was the core group destined to go all the way to the Pacific Ocean and back. The remaining crew members were organized into two messes: seven engagés under Patroon Baptist Dechamps, and six privates under Corporal Richard Warvington.

The duties of the sergeants were then spelled out in extreme detail to develop a rank of command that the men would follow for the remainder of the expedition.

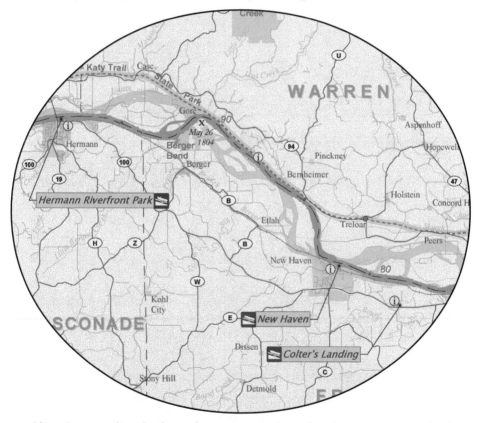

If you're traveling by boat, be sure to explore the picturesque stretch of Missouri River between Hermann and New Haven. Visit the Hermann Riverfront Park to use their excellent boat ramp or to simply enjoy the view. If you don't have a boat, ask someone for a ride!

Hermann, Missouri

Hermann is best known for its area wineries, such as Stone Hill, shown above and at left. Be sure to visit the other area wineries as well, to truly get a "taste" of Missouri wine country.

Today's Trail

Explore Hermann, Missouri

Hermann has remarkably preserved early German architecture, great shops and more than 40 bed & breakfasts. This historic German community, founded in 1836, is known primarily for its yearly Maifest, Wurstfest and Octoberfest weekend celebrations. However, there is plenty to do in this town throughout the year. Numerous Hermann restaurants—both German in origin and otherwise—are sure to please any palate. Plan to tour the large historic district, which retains many fine examples of early German architecture.

Take the cellar tour at Stone Hill Winery—Missouri's largest. Be sure to visit other area wineries as well. Hermanhof Winery, OakGlenn Winery and Adam Puchta Winery are also "must visits." Call the Missouri Grape & Wine Program for a complete listing and a map of the 40-plus wineries located throughout the state: (800) 392-WINE.

(800) 932-8687 • www.hermannmo.com

*The view of the Missouri River bridge from
high atop Hermann's bluffs is postcard perfect.*

*Visit the Deutschheim State Historic Site in Hermann
for an excellent overview of the area's German settlers.*

Expedition Entry
Near the confluence with the Gasconade River
Sunday, May 27, 1804

As the Corps is setting out, they encounter two canoes heading downstream, loaded with beaver, elk, deer skins and buffalo robes from the Omaha nation. Later in the day they see four rafts pass by loaded with furs and pelts from the Pawnee and Grand Osage. They camp that night on a willow island at the mouth of the Gasconade River. George Shannon kills a deer that evening. The crew makes 15 and a half miles progress today.

Expedition Entry
Near Gasconade, Missouri
Monday, May 28, 1804

After enduring a hard rain all night long, the Captains find that due to the carelessness of the eight French hands on the large pirogue, many things have gotten wet, and some tobacco has spoiled. The items are set out to dry. The day remains so cloudy that no observations can be taken. The river has begun to rise.

Morel Mushroom

May 29, 1804

Expedition Entry

Near Bluffton & Grand Bluffs Conservation Area
Tuesday, May 29, 1804

Four hunters are dispatched with orders to return by noon. The crew have the pirogues loaded and ready to depart by 4 p.m. when the Captains find that one of the hunters, Joseph Whitehouse, has not returned. The Corps is determined to proceed on and they leave one pirogue to wait for him. Leaving camp at 4:30 p.m., the crew makes 4 miles of progress.

Upon his return, Whitehouse says he has discovered a cave while out hunting. He describes it as one of the most remarkable he has ever seen. The location of this cave, either in Callaway or Montgomery County, remains a mystery. After Clark hears several guns fire downriver (perhaps signaling that Whitehouse has returned), the keelboat answers with a discharge from the bow's swivel gun. The river continues to rise. Lewis makes observations on an island opposite the mouth of the Gasconade River. "The musquetors are verry bad," Clark notes.

Today's Trail

Explore Bluffton, Missouri

Today Bluffton consists of little more than Steamboat Junction, a popular campground with limited services for Katy Trail cyclists: (314) 831-4807. However, the towering 200-foot-tall bluffs make this a popular section of the Katy Trail to explore, since the trail hugs the river's edge, far away from the bustle of Hwy 94 traffic. When pedaling this stretch, you'll also pass beside Grand Bluffs Conservation Area and Tate Island. Be sure to check out the conservation department overlook here that offers an excellent vantage point from atop these bluffs. The tall bluffs here have been noted by traders and explorers since 1728, when it was first recorded: "Rocher le plus haut de la Route" (the highest rock on the route).

Expedition Entry
Near Little Tavern Creek
Wednesday, May 30, 1804

Despite another night of incessant rain and surely little sleep, the crew makes 17 miles of progress today. They pass Montbrun's Tavern Cave located at the mouth of Little Tavern Creek. They report that the river is rising very fast.

Today's Trail
Explore Portland, Missouri

The portion of Katy Trail that passes through Portland is shaded by towering cottonwood trees. The trail here offers several nice pull-offs with expansive Missouri River views. A local tavern offers cold beer, great hamburgers and a pool table all within a stone's throw of the trail and boat ramp.

> *The largest fish known to have been caught on the Missouri River, a blue channel cat weighing 315 pounds, was caught just below Portland in 1866.*

A relic of river travel near Mokane awaits high water to take it on one last trip down the Mighty Mo. With any luck, it will continue out to sea for a Viking funeral and entry into Valhalla.

May 31, 1804

Expedition Entry
Near Auxvasse Creek
Thursday, May 31, 1804

Clark talks with a Frenchman trader, a squaw and their child, heading downriver with a raft loaded with bear hides and small pelts. They are coming down from trading with the Grand Osage Indians on the Arkansas River in Kansas. The trader had delivered a letter to the Osage telling them that the Americans now had possession of this region, which was not believed by the Osage.

Clark writes, "Several rats of Considerable Size was Cought in the woods to day." This rat was the Eastern wood rat, the first newly discovered species of the expedition.

Today's Trail
Explore Bonnots Mill, Missouri

When visiting Mid-Missouri, Bonnots Mill is a must-visit. Hemmed in by steep hills and bluffs along the Osage River, Bonnots Mill offers visitors a nice reward for taking the back roads: an historic inn, two restaurants and a nice vantage point that overlooks the confluence of the Osage and Missouri Rivers (at the Bonnots Mill Parish Hall).

This is my favorite roadtrip destination on motorcycle trips. Take the lazily winding and curvaceous Hwy 179 from up near Boonville down to Jefferson City, enjoy the stops, then scoot about 20 miles east to spend the night at the Dauphine Hotel. Please note this is generally considered a Thursday through Sunday town. Call the inn for more information: (573) 897-4144.

Bonnots Mill is the successor to two previous villages, French Village and Cote Sans Dessein, both of which succumbed to river encroachment. The first European settlement in the area, Cote Sans Dessein was begun as a

Bonnots Mill offers visitors a nice reward for exploring the backroads: a historic inn, shown at right, and picturesque rivertown charm that is pure Missouri.

trading post by French-Canadians for dealing with Osage, Shawnee and Delaware Indians.

The Dauphine Hotel has been welcoming travelers along the Missouri River since 1875. The hotel started as a two-room farmhouse built by an American settler in the 1840s. The location was at a French settlement called Dauphine (its name prior to becoming Bonnots Mill). The founder of Dauphine, Felix Bonnot, came from France in the 1840s and eventually purchased the farmhouse and land. In 1870, he sold the house and land to relatives of his wife, Lucienne Party. The Partys then built the Dauphine Hotel, which was open for business in 1875 and is one of Missouri's oldest lodging establishments.

The Dauphine Hotel is listed on the National Register of Historic Places and is part of the Bonnots Mill National Historic District. The Dauphine Hotel offers six guestrooms, each furnished with antique dressers and iron beds original to the hotel. A full country breakfast is served in the large family-style kitchen as well as the adjacent dining room. Innkeepers Sandra and Scott Holder pride themselves on offering a comfortable and very casual atmosphere in one of the most authentic old hotels west of the Mississippi.

The Dauphine is the only hotel in the tiny town of Bonnots Mill, originally servicing river travelers and farmers bringing grain to the mill, and then the railroad traffic. Salesmen called "drummers" would arrive via steamboat or the railroad and stay at the Dauphine. They would sell their wares in an open market on the street in front of the hotel.

The Partys eventually sold the Dauphine Hotel and about half a dozen owners passed through its doors until the Verdot family purchased the hotel in 1890. Adelaide and Alex Verdot and their four daughters, Constance, Lizzy, Louise, and Annie, lived in the three family rooms of the Dauphine. Alex was a county judge and had a number of other businesses while the women ran the hotel. Little changed on the outside of the Dauphine in 120 years. Adelaide died in the early 1920s and Alex in 1928. By that time, one daughter, Constance, was married and had moved to Kansas. The three remaining sisters continued to live in the hotel and operate it.

By 1930, they made the decision to shut down the Dauphine as a regular hotel, although they occasionally rented rooms to long-term boarders. The reason for the closure was twofold: U.S. Highway 50 was finally paved by 1930, which diverted most traffic away from Bonnots Mill. Furthermore, the Great Depression was in full swing by then, so what little commerce and traffic that had passed through town virtually ceased to exist.

The three sisters, or "the Girls" as they were known by most area residents, lived in the hotel for the remainder of their lives. They never married and all lived well into their 90s. The last sister died in 1970 and their nephew purchased the Dauphine Hotel. Unfortunately, many of the original antiques were either sold or given away. However, many items original to the Dauphine, namely the iron beds and the dining room table, are original and probably predate the Verdots' ownership.

In 1979, Bob and Barbara Bregant purchased the Dauphine and began a 15-year renovation that resulted in all of the upstairs bedrooms, the kitchen and the dining room being refinished. Scott and Sandra Holder purchased it in 1994. Guests will be hard pressed to find another B&B as authentic and yet as comfortable as the Dauphine Hotel.

(877) 901-4144 • www.dauphinehotel.com

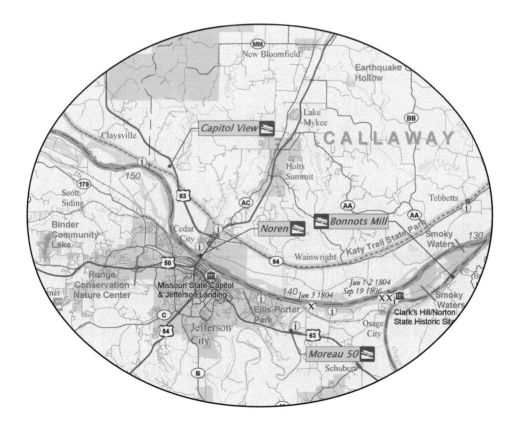

June 2, 1804

Expedition Entry

Clark's Hill/Norton State Historic Site
At the confluence of the Osage & Missouri Rivers
Saturday, June 2, 1804

This promontory, located high above the Missouri River, is mentioned in Clark's journal, "from this pt. which commands both rivers I had a delightfull prospect of the Missouries up & down, also the Osage River up."

Today's Trail

Explore Clark's Hill/Norton State Historic Site
Near Osage City, Missouri

Clark's Hill is one of the most pleasant and historically significant stops along the Lewis & Clark Trail in Missouri. You can stand here and know with certainty that you have indeed walked in Clark's footsteps. This site, recently donated to the state by Bill and Carol Norton, is now open to the public. It was named for Captain Clark, who climbed to the top of the promontory and admired the panoramic view of the Osage and Missouri Rivers. He made his daily observations here on June 2, 1804. As you slowly climb toward the overlook, take a few moments to forget about today. Try to arrive on the hilltop and see the extensive river view through Clark's eyes.

(800) 334-6946 • www.mostateparks.com

Expedition Entry

Near the Moreau River
Sunday, June 3, 1804

The Corps makes five miles of progress today. They camp at the mouth of Moreau River, where Clark sees fresh signs of Indians having crossed here. Two deer were killed today. Clark complains of a sore throat. "& am Tormented with Musquetors & Small ticks," he writes.

Habitation of Graham Cave dates back to 10,000 years ago.

Today's Trail
Explore Graham Cave State Park
Danville, Missouri

If you are touring Missouri's Lewis & Clark Trail via Highway I-70, be sure to take the Williamsburg exit to grab lunch at Crane's Country Store, then take the Danville exit to explore Graham Cave State Park. Habitation of Graham Cave dates back to 10,000 years ago. Today, you can visit this shallow shelter cave and look through a fence to read interpretive signs that point out the locations of interesting archaeological finds.

Surrounding Graham Cave are 356 acres of rolling forested land with several hiking trails. Playgrounds and picnic shelters make the park an ideal place for a stop. A wooded camping area offers basic and electric campsites, restrooms and hot showers.

Nearby, a boat ramp on the Loutre River provides access for boating and fishing. Other area highlights include the Baker Plantation Home, the Crane Country Store in Williamsburg and Fulton's Iron Curtain sculpture. Visit the Heart of Missouri Visitors Center north of the I-70 Kingdom City exit for information.

(573) 564-3476 • www.mostateparks.com/grahamcave.htm

The Missouri Capitol fronts the Missouri River. The Veterans Memorial pool is shown in the foreground of this photograph. Also nearby is a bronze relief of the signing of the Louisiana Purchase. After touring the Capitol, be sure to exit on the river side to take in the sweeping river view. A towering bronze of Thomas Jefferson is located on the opposite side of the Capitol.

Today's Trail

Explore Jefferson City, Missouri

A tour of Missouri's capital city offers many insights into early pioneer life. Located right on the Missouri River, Jefferson City's sites are directly tied to the evolution of river trade and the story of Lewis & Clark. Out in front of the Capitol is a larger-than-life bronze of Thomas Jefferson. Inside the Capitol, you'll find bronze busts of Sacagawea, Meriwether Lewis and William Clark. Tour the State Capitol's State Museum and be sure to take their guided tour that includes famous Thomas Hart Benton murals. Tour the Jefferson Landing State Historic Site, where steamboats brought immigrants who settled the area. The nearby Runge Conservation Area has trails and great kid-friendly wildlife displays. The North Jefferson Katy Trail trailhead is located directly across the Missouri River. A ten-mile pedal west will bring you to Hartsburg, or pedal east 12 miles to visit tiny Tebbetts, where you will find a deli and the Turner Katy Trail Shelter youth hostel: (800) 575-2322.

(800) 769-4183 • www.visitjeffersoncity.com

*The Capitol's State Museum offers an excellent overview
of the many faces and forces that molded Missouri.*

Above, the North Jefferson Trailhead offers easy access to the heart of the Katy Trail State Park. Below, the Jefferson Landing Historic Site recounts the early days of river travel.

The Amtrak stop is here too, offering easy access to other Lewis & Clark Trail towns, such as St. Louis (Kirkwood), Washington, Independence and Hermann.

(800) USA-RAIL • www.amtrak.com

Fellow Missouri guidebook authors Diana Lambdin Meyer (left) and Katie Van Luchene take a break from the trail at Central Dairy Ice Cream in Jefferson City.

Let's face it, there's nothing better than a triple scoop of Mocha Blaster ice cream to help your brain process all of this history stuff. So stop at Central Dairy Ice Cream, a Mid-Missouri institution, serving ice cream since 1936. If you are one of those Seize-the-Moment people, order the Rock 'n Roll—eight scoops of your four favorite ice creams with four toppings and nuts. It costs less than the price of a movie ticket and has enough calories to power a Third World country. They also serve hot dogs and other fixings. At 610 Madison Street. (573) 635-6148.

Digging History
One Canoe at a Time

*T*hese guys really dig history. Using a mix of period tools, such as adzes, hatchets and axes, along with hour upon hour of their own can-do spirit, they're getting dugout canoes out of the history books and back onto the river.

The Lewis & Clark Dugout Canoe Crew is made up of staff volunteers from the Missouri Department of Conservation. They have built replicas of the canoes used by the Corps of Discovery. The early 1800s were a time when, as one person put it, "canoes made out of cottonwood trees were Cadillacs and the Missouri River was the highway."

Tom Ronk, a crew member, says the dugout canoe was "the unsung hero of the expedition." He says the Corps used dugouts on about 80-percent of their riverway travels to the Pacific Ocean and back. Historians believe the Corps used as many as 20 dugout canoes during their expedition.

Turning a log into a canoe is tedious business. It took six members of the canoe crew six days to build one dugout canoe. In that same amount of time, Lewis & Clark and their fellow explorers could whittle out about four.

So far, the canoe crew has finished four dugouts, with another four in the works. Each one is a real piece of art. The one shown here is named The Osage. It's a 28-foot-long 3,000-pounder able to float the Missouri River just like its predecessors. The canoes seat five or six people in their hollowed-out cockpit. The canoe crew put their boats on the Missouri River every chance they get. They say the canoes are remarkably stable since all the weight is on the bottom, but that they're a lot harder to maneuver than today's fiberglass canoes.

Expect to see their crew and canoes at various events up and down the trail in 2004 and beyond. Contact the Missouri Department of Conservation for information: (573) 751-4115.

Jefferson City, Missouri

Bull Rock Historic Site offers a shaded vantage point from which to view this scenic stretch of river. Opposite page: Cara and Larry Stauffer's renovated farmhouse serves as Native Stone's tasting room.

Today's Trail
Explore Bull Rock Historic Site
Jefferson City, Missouri

Be sure to visit Native Stone Winery & Bull Rock Brewery—named after Bull Rock, a knob of limestone long noted by river travelers. On the winery's extensive premises are their tasting room, dining area and the Bull Rock Historic Site. There is a one-mile hike over rolling hills to get to the site's river view and it's worth it. Top-notch Lewis & Clark signage is sprinkled at just the right intervals along the hike to allow you to take a breather in the shade without looking like you need it. Sample their great wines and beers and enjoy a lunch inside or outdoors. Call ahead for hours. Native Stone Winery is located ten minutes northwest of Jefferson City. From Jefferson City, take Hwy 50 west to Hwy 179, exit right. Go approximately nine miles on Hwy 179 north/west. Pass over Meadow Creek Bridge. Native Stone Road is on your right. (573) 584-8600. www.nativestonewinery.com.

June 4, 1804

Expedition Entry
Between Jefferson City & Hartsburg, Missouri
Monday, June 4, 1804

"A fair day," Clark writes. Three hunters are dispatched. The mast breaks after running the boat under a tree, probably near Gray's Creek. They pass Cedar Island, covered with large cedar trees. They pass a small creek which they "named Nightingale Creek from a Bird of that discription which Sang for us all last night, and is the first of the Kind I ever heard." They also pass the future site of Jefferson City.

During the day, they stop opposite a point called Batue a De charm (Bature Ducharme) at the mouth of Zoncar (Joncar) Creek, probably today's Workman Creek. Clark explores the area, crossing a rush bottom, then ascending a hill 170 feet high to check out a report by one of the party of finding lead ore, but Clark finds none.

Clark writes "Some delightfull Land, with a jentle assent about the Creek, well timbered, Oake, Ash, walnut &c." Clark notes finding a mound on top of the hill about six feet high and about 100 acres of dead trees. There was an extensive "encompassing" cave about 50 feet down from the top of the hill. He goes out on a rock projecting over the river (today's Sugar Loaf Rock) and has an unencumbered view of the river for 20 to 30 miles. Hunters kill seven deer today. The crew makes 17 and a half miles of progress upriver today.

Today's Trail
Explore Hartsburg, Missouri

Between Columbia and Jefferson City there are several towns to visit along Katy Trail State Park, including Easley, Wilton and Hartsburg. Hartsburg, population 118, is a popular launching point for Katy Trail cyclists. It is one of Mid-Missouri's most charismatic rivertowns, offering visitors an historic bed and breakfast, a bicycle shop, a winery and The Hitching Post, which is best known for the informal folk and bluegrass music jam session held every Sunday afternoon.

The bluffs along this section rise high above the Missouri River. If you can manage to be on the trail near sunset, you will have a great view of these majestic rock faces bathed in warm light as the sun's last rays wash over the valley. Another thing to see along this stretch of trail are the American bald eagles during the fall, winter and early spring. Even without a pair of binoculars, watching these birds soar over the river is a memorable experience.

Several events are held in Hartsburg throughout the year. The Fish Fry in July and the Hartsburg Pumpkin Festival the second weekend in October are two of Hartsburg's biggest events. Hundreds of families come down the hill into this river town one weekend each fall for the Pumpkin Festival. Come by bike via the Katy Trail to avoid the traffic. (Don't forget your Burley cart to haul the kids and the pumpkin!) Play games, enjoy live music, drink some cider and visit dozens of booths and activities—all the while looking to find a perfect Halloween pumpkin before you leave.

While in Hartsburg, plan to stay at the historic Globe Hotel Bed & Breakfast, a restored 1893 hotel just steps from the trail and the rest of town: (573) 657-4529. And be sure to visit Thornhill Winery: (573) 657-4295. For camping information, call the American Legion at (573) 636-7514 and Bush Landing at (573) 657-2609.

Heading east, you'll enjoy 12 miles of scenery leading to the North Jefferson City Trailhead and beyond. (The Katy Trail and the state capitol are on opposite sides of the Missouri River.)

June 5, 1804

Today's Trail

Explore Wilton, Missouri

This tiny river hamlet is best known for the Riverview Traders Store, full of Native American crafts created by Robert and Maggie Riesenmy. They also offer snacks, camping supplies, drinks and the only camping spot on the entire Katy Trail where you can spend the night in a tipi. Call the Riverview Traders Store for more information: (573) 657-1095.

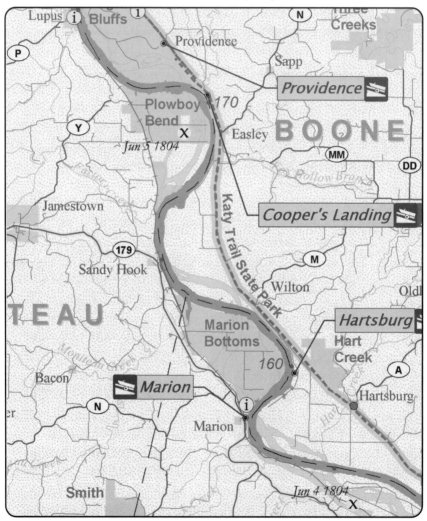

The Katy Trail in Mid-Missouri offers easy access to unique camping, great B&Bs, fun annual festivals and gorgeous river views.

Maggie also illustrated the *Katy Trail Nature Guide*, drawing more than 400 of the most commonly seen wildflowers, trees, birds and wildlife of the river valley. For information on the book, call Pebble Publishing: (573) 698-3903.

Expedition Entry
Near Lupus & Easley, Missouri
Tuesday, June 5, 1804

Today the crew jerks the venison. They pass a raft with two Frenchmen coming from the Kansas River, where they wintered and had caught a great quantity of beaver, which they unfortunately lost due to the burning of the plains. Two miles above the Little Manitou (Moniteau) Creek, the Corps passes a projecting rock with a figure painted on it (shown above), which Clark calls a "Deavel" due to its horns or antlers. York, Clark's slave, swims to an island to gather greens. Clark writes "a fair wind... our mast being broke by accidence provented our takeing the advantage of it." The hunters discover signs of a war party of about ten men, which Clark assumes were probably the "Saukees" on their way to war against the Osage Nation. They pass an area where the current divides between four islands. Getting upriver was excessively hard, yet 12 and a half miles progress are made today.

Spend a night in a tipi at Wilton's small campground.

June 6, 1804

Today's Trail
Explore Cooper's Landing
Near Easley, Missouri

Cooper's Landing, located just upriver from Easley, is a popular hangout for Missouri River rats and Katy cyclists. Cooper's Landing often hosts live music in the summer months and is the only boat ramp in Mid-Missouri where you can refuel your boat. Great riverside sunset views, primitive camping, lodging and wonderful Thai food are to be found here. Expect crowds until pretty late, so either bring ear plugs for camping or join the party!

(573) 657-2544 • www.cooperslanding.net

Today's Trail
Explore Lupus, Missouri

Lupus, population 29, is easily accessible to boats traveling the Lewis & Clark Trail. Lupus is for river rats what Graceland is for Elvis fans. I'm not sure exactly what that means, but if you're a river rat, you'll understand.

This small town has fought the Missouri River's tendency to leave its banks in an interesting way—by raising the houses, some up to ten feet, rather than trying to use conventional levees to keep the flood waters out. Their determination to hold onto this patch of paradise is almost palpable in the air.

Visit local potter Diane Denman at Wolf's Point Studio. Inspired by the delicate beauty of inherited family lace, Diana uses lace and plant impressions to create large free-form bowls, trays and wall pockets that are elegant and unique.

If you're in Mid-Missouri in October, be sure to put a canoe in the river at Rocheport and float down to the annual Lupus chili festival, which has become a mini-Woodstock type event with live music and great chili. Although attempts have been made to curb the event somewhat, you can't close the gates on Graceland.

Expedition Entry
Eagle Bluffs Conservation Area
Columbia, Missouri
Wednesday, June 6, 1804

After fixing the mast from their June 4 mishap, the crew sets out at 7 a.m. They pass Saline Creek (today known as Petite Saline Creek) and note many licks (or salt springs).

The Corps also passes the mouth of Perche Creek (Split Rock Creek), near present-day Columbia. Here Captain Lewis took meridian readings, while Captain Clark noted a projecting rock that had a hole or cave through its point. While Clark's journal refers to it as "Split Rock," several other accounts from the early 1800s refer to the feature as "Roche Piercee" or other variations of the French term for "pierced rock." Today, Pierced Rock (or Roche Piercee Natural Arch) is located within the Eagle Bluffs Conservation Area. You can view Pierced Rock by riding the Katy Trail to mile post 166.9. There is also a wayside interpretive sign near the mouth of Perche Creek that tells the story.

Clark writes, "The Countrey for Several miles below is good, on the top of the high land back is also tolerable land... Some buffalow Sign to day... I am Still verry unwell with a Sore throat & head ake." The Corps makes 14 miles today.

Today's Trail

Explore Eagle Bluffs Conservation Area
Columbia, Missouri

The Katy Trail passes through a portion of the Eagle Bluffs Conservation Area. Here you can see Pierced Rock Natural Arch, described by Clark in his journal (see previous page) by riding the Katy Trail to mile post 166.9. There is also a wayside interpretive sign near the mouth of Perche Creek that tells the story. Photography, bird watching and fishing are popular activities here.

Located south of Columbia, Eagle Bluffs offers easy driving and hiking access to expansive river bottoms composed of man-made wetlands, which were created to help offset the loss of nearly 90-percent of Missouri's historical wetlands. The area uses treated wastewater from the city of Columbia as a primary water source for the wetlands.

Several parking areas offer an up-close look at the Mighty Missouri and the tall bluffs on the other side of the river. The Missouri River once flowed through the area and the steamboat *Plowboy* is believed to be buried under the silt on the area.

(573) 445-3882 • www.conservation.state.mo.us

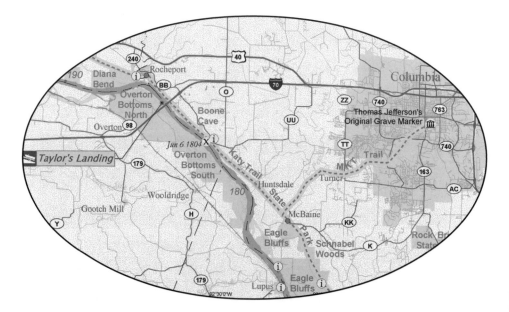

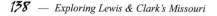

The picturesque columns are located on the quad at the heart of the University of Missouri–Columbia campus.

Today's Trail

Explore Columbia, Missouri

Often called "College Town U.S.A.," Columbia is a popular home base for exploring all of Mid-Missouri's Lewis & Clark related sites. In addition to more than 26 hotels, there are also several bed and breakfasts, many gourmet restaurants, an extensive variety of shops, camping and RV hookups, museums and more.

Located on the University of Missouri–Columbia quadrangle, near the columns, is a bronze sculpture of Thomas Jefferson, as well as his original grave marker. MU received this grave marker when the original was replaced many years ago, since MU was the first public university founded in Jefferson's Louisiana Purchase territory. Also nearby is the Museum of Anthropology, which features many Native American artifacts from throughout Missouri and beyond.

MU's music department has a traveling opera about the Lewis & Clark Expedition, called *Corps of Discovery: A Musical Journey.* Call (573) 884-1604 for information.

Be sure to visit Bluestem Missouri Crafts located on Ninth Street. Bluestem highlights many members of the Best of Missouri Hands, with art that ranges from glass to pottery to textiles and more.

If you are looking for grub, one favorite is Shakespeare's Pizza, also located on Ninth Street. Even after leaving Columbia and eating pizza from all over the world, many MU grads swear that "Shakes" still holds the title of best pizza. Other local favorites include Main Squeeze, which features organic, fresh foods and the best all-natural shakes in town. Also nearby are Lakota Coffee, Cherry Street Artisan, Booche's, Panera Bread and a dozen other great local restaurants. For breakfast, order the Stretch at the Broadway Diner, 22 S. Fourth Street.

When you visit Columbia, pedal the MK&T Fitness Trail down to McBaine where it meets up with the Katy Trail, then pedal your way to Easley, Huntsdale or Rocheport for the day.

(573) 875-1231 • www.visitcolumbiamo.com

A bronze Thomas Jefferson can be found on the quad sipping a mocha and cramming for a poli-sci mid-term. Also nearby is a Beetle Bailey bronze— a tribute to artist and MU grad Mort Walker. While you're here, get directions to Lowry Mall (within walking distance) to see MU's huge glass tiger mosaic (near McDonald's).

Today's Trail

Explore Rock Bridge Memorial State Park
Columbia, Missouri

While walking the half-mile Devil's Icebox boardwalk, you'll see an underground stream, spring and sinkhole and pass both under and over the rock bridge seen in the photograph above. Your kids will love it! Fifteen miles of trail traverse this 2,200-acre park. Check their events calendar for guided walks and children's programs. This is one stop you'll want to make.

Sign up for the epic eight-hour Devil's Icebox cave tour (a month in advance). Caving trips are offered in the spring and fall. I was an assistant trip leader on cave tours here while in college and I highly recommend the trip. The first half-mile of the cave is a water passage, which requires carrying in a canoe. You paddle and then carry the canoe over several portages. Then you lie flat in your canoe to fit through a 15-foot-long low spot. It's a lot of fun, especially if you go in at dusk when bats are flying right into your face, turning at the very last possible second, illuminated only by your headlamp. The rest of the trip is spent walking through spacious passages with assorted slippery mud, steep banks and wading through cold water.

(573) 449-7402 • www.mostateparks.com/rockbridge.htm

Katfish Katy's is a biker's oasis, located 6.6 miles south of Rocheport on the Katy Trail at Katy Trail mile marker 171.7.

Today's Trail
Explore Huntsdale, Missouri

Be sure to visit Katfish Katy's Convenience store, a small depot-styled addition to the Katy Trail scene. This wonderfully stocked store includes everything from cameras to groceries and fishing supplies. Some of the nicest riverside camping in Mid-Missouri is to be found here, atop the shaded levee right beside the Mighty Mo. A nice shower house and restrooms make this a top notch secluded camping option. There is also a lodging option in Huntsdale called Katy's Little Lodge at 8809 Sarr Street. Call (573) 446-0664.

The boat ramp here is as good as it gets—great in high and low water, even when other ramps in the area are unusable. A popular float is from Rocheport to Huntsdale (2 – 4 hours). Bring your camping gear and have your bikes stowed somewhere so you can pedal back up to Rocheport to run your vehicle shuttle.

(573) 447-3939 • www.katfishkatys.com

Today's Trail

Explore Boone Cave Conservation Area
Rocheport, Missouri

This scenic area is currently closed by road, but Katy Trail access only primitive camping (no services) is allowed here through 2006. The immense mouth of Boone Cave is the scenic highlight of this area. Tucked into a steeply banked alcove, the towering cave opening is a great photography stop, with a nice cool breeze and a shallow rocky creek to keep the young ones entertained. The cave entrance is gated to protect endangered bat habitat. Contact the Eagle Bluffs Conservation Area for more information: (573) 445-3882.

Tucked into a steeply banked alcove, the towering Boone Cave opening is a great photography stop, with a nice cool breeze and a shallow rocky creek to keep the young ones entertained.

Visit the Missouri River Communities Network website and print out their Mid-Missouri driving tours. They also maintain a list of bicentennial events to help you plan your trip: www.moriver.org

Region Review

From Rocheport to Lexington, Missouri

June 7 – 19, 1804

*T*hroughout this stretch of river, Clark frequently uses the terms "butiful" and "mosquetors." He makes daily observations of plentiful bear, deer and turkey. Despite the beautiful views, the boat crews are plagued with difficult stretches of river that test the mettle of this newly formed crew. The crew's determination in the face of the virtually impenetrable Missouri River brought Clark to write during this stretch, "I can Say with Confidence that our party is not inferior to any that was ever on the waters of the Misso[rr]ie."

He goes on to say just a week later, "our party is ever ready to encounter any fatigue for the promotion of the enterprise."

Expedition Entry

Near Rocheport, Missouri
Thursday, June 7, 1804

The "good quallity" flint, also known as chert, can still be seen along the bluffs near Rocheport.

The Corps sets out early and explores the mouth of a creek called Big Manito or Manitou (now known as Moniteau Creek) at present-day Rocheport. Clark mentions the high bluffs on the starboard side and passing a painted part of the projecting rock. Clark writes, "A Short distance above the mouth of this Creek, is Several Courious Paintings and Carveing in the projecting rock, of Limestone inlade with white, red & blue flint of a verry good quallity, the Indians have taken of this flint great quantities."

Clark also mentions "We landed at this Inscription and found it a Den of rattle Snakes, we had not landed three minutes before three verry large Snakes wer observed on the Crevises of the rocks & Killed."

Seeing some buffalo sign, two hunters leave to hunt. Lewis and six men follow the Moniteau Creek to a lick (salt springs). Clark writes, "the water runs out of the bank & not verry Strong... 3 to 500 gallons for a bushell." The hunters return with three bear (the first bears killed on the expedition). The crew camps at the mouth of Bonne Femme Creek, after making 14 miles of progress today.

The crew of the Discovery Expedition of St. Charles rows
replicas of Lewis & Clark's white and red pirogues down the
Missouri River near the Manitou Bluffs at Rocheport.

Names to Know
Manitou Bluffs

he towering bluffs along the Missouri River
at Rocheport have long been a favorite sight for
explorers and river boatmen, and more recently,
photographers, paddlers and cyclists. The bluffs here
are called the Manitou Bluffs.

These bluffs are considered sacred by several tribes that
once lived in the area. See Clark's journal entry for June 7,
1804, on the previous page.

"Moniteau" is a French derivative of "Manitou," the Indian
word for Great Spirit, hence the naming of Moniteau Creek that
flows through Rocheport, near the Katy Trail Tunnel. A very
faded pictograph can be seen a few miles south of Rocheport
above the Lewis & Clark Cave (about Katy Trail mile marker
175), otherwise known as Torbett Spring. From the cave

entrance (well marked by a Conservation Department sign), look 25 – 40 feet to the left and up approximately 35 – 50 feet. The maroon-colored pictograph of a "V" with a dot is right beside the bottom edge of the left bow of a prominent fracture impression. The crescent moon and dot symbol is thought to mark the water source below.

This appears to be the only pictograph to survive the progress of man, since many located under overhangs were blasted off to prevent train accidents and to create rock to channelize the Missouri River.

On June 7, 1804, Clark writes, "A Short distance above the mouth of this Creek is Several Courious Paintings and Carveing in the projecting rock of Limestone..." Above are the pictographs he recorded in his journal that day at what would become Rocheport.

Rocheport offers easy access to the heart of Katy Trail country.
The fine gravel surface makes it easy to pedal a variety of bikes.

A storm-weathered cedar grows high above Rocheport.
The Missouri River, bluffs and the Katy Trail are seen in the distance.

Today's Trail
Explore Rocheport, Missouri

The small river town of Rocheport (French for "port of rocks"), is often called the Gateway to the Katy Trail. The scenic bluff-lined Katy Trail, the panoramic Missouri River views, a blufftop timber-frame winery, bike rental, several award-winning bed and breakfasts and antique shops all offer an inviting weekend getaway in this small, walkable river town.

Walking through the old train tunnel blasted through solid rock is a particular highlight of this stretch of trail. The bluff the tunnel goes through is thought to be where the pictographs were noted by William Clark (see previous pages). The construction of the railroad tunnel surely led to their destruction. At the tunnel entrance, be sure to walk towards the river on the wooden walkway. Steps lead up to a very nice bluff overlook. This is a good spot for a picnic.

Area bed & breakfasts include the School House B&B (voted the favorite Missouri B&B by readers of *Rural Missouri* magazine), the Yates House B&B, and Katy O'Neil's Bed &

Visit Art & Antiques to see George Robb hand forge ironwork in his blacksmith shop. The Les Bourgeois Blufftop Bistro is known for its excellent food and river views.

Bikefest. Bike rentals, a local museum and several outstanding restaurants will round out your visit to Rocheport. Be sure to visit the Pebble Publishing bookstore, operated by the author of this book. It stocks a ton of Lewis & Clark books, Missouri and river history, guidebooks and more. Rocheport businesses tend to be open predominantly from Wednesday through Sunday, although some businesses are open more than that.

(573) 698-3903 • www.rocheport.com

Today's Trail

Explore Diana Bend & Franklin Island Conservation Areas
Rocheport, Missouri

The Diana Bend Conservation Area allows Katy Trail State Park visitors a chance to view firsthand a portion of the Missouri River floodplain in the process of restoration. View herons, migratory shorebirds and waterfowl from a walkway and wheelchair-accessible viewing blind. An overlook platform, located high above Rocheport's old railroad tunnel, offers a panoramic river valley view. Explore both sites via a walkway to the left of the Katy Trail at the railroad tunnel in Rocheport.

One of the most popular boat accesses between Boonville and Rocheport is located within the 1,616-acre Franklin Island Conservation Area, which sits between the Missouri River and Bonne Femme Creek. Franklin Island is the site of the expedition's camp on June 7, 1804.

(573) 884-6861 • www.conservation.state.mo.us/atlas

Enjoy a panoramic view of the Missouri River from the blufftop Les Bourgeois Winery & Bistro in Rocheport. There is also a nearby blufftop viewing platform that offers similar views accessible via a wooden walkway located at the entrance to the Katy Trail Tunnel in Rocheport.

Today's Trail

Explore New Franklin, Missouri

New Franklin is close to the original site of Franklin, where the Santa Fe Trail began. New Franklin is also known as the town where "the four trails meet," because the Lewis & Clark Trail, the Katy Trail, the Santa Fe Trail and the Boonslick Road all pass through town.

This small community offers easy access to the Katy Roundhouse Restaurant & Campground, which is located in a historic Missouri, Kansas & Texas Railroad depot and switching station. The memorabilia on the walls recalls the heyday of the Katy Railroad. Now a popular destination for Katy cyclists, the restaurant serves dinner on Friday and Saturday nights. The old "turn table," which allowed the engineers to pivot engines into various bays, is located in the center of the roundhouse complex.

(660) 848-2232 • www.katyroundhouse.com

Be sure to say hello to Katy, the Roundhouse's resident canine. The Katy Roundhouse is a true biker's oasis. It is located directly on the Katy Trail and offers an excellent camping & RV experience, along with great dinners and an incredible collection of Katy Railroad memorabilia.

Spend a night at Rivercene B&B, a mansion built by Riverboat Captain Kinney. It opens a unique door into the opulent past of the riverboat era.

Today's Trail

Explore Boonville, Missouri

Boonville is best known for its yearly Big Muddy Folk Festival held at Thespian Hall. However, other festivities can be found here throughout the year. Visit the Chamber of Commerce in the MK&T Depot at the Katy Trailhead for information.

The Old Cobblestone Street Park under the Boonslick Bridge is considered to be the oldest paved street west of St. Louis. At this park are the highwater marks from 1844, 1903 and 1993. Interpretive signs make this well worth the visit. Take a walk across the bridge on the wide pedestrian lane for a great photo-op of the Missouri River. Be sure to also visit Harley Park for its panoramic view of the Big Muddy.

Connoisseurs of early architecture need to tour High Street, which parallels the river, for a look at some early Victorian homes. Right across the river, Rivercene Bed & Breakfast, built by an early riverboat captain, is a Mid-Missouri treasure steeped in riverlore: (800) 531-0862. www.rivercene.com.

(660) 882-2721 • www.c-magic.com/boonvill/

*Arrow Rock's Lyceum Theater is considered
"Missouri's Best Theater" by readers of* Rural Missouri.

Expedition Entry
Near Arrow Rock, Missouri
Friday, June 8, 1804

*Today the Corps proceeds 12 miles upriver, passing two
willow islands and a small creek. Nine miles into their day's
progress, they pass the Mine River, known today as the
Lamine River. "This river is about 70 yards wide at its mouth
and is Said to be navagable for Perogues 80 or 90 ms. The west
branch passes near the place where the Little osage Village
formerly stood on the Missouries… The french inform that
Lead Ore has been found in defferent parts of this river," Clark
wrote. Clark and Sergeant Floyd explore the Lamine for a
mile, and find it sufficiently watered with small streams. The
Corps' hunters bring in five deer today, although incessant
rains keep them from cooking.*

Today's Trail

Explore Arrow Rock, Missouri

A stroll along Arrow Rock's streets captures the ambience of Missouri's pioneer days. The early stone gutters, wooden sidewalks, historic Tavern Restaurant and area visitors center all offer a firsthand opportunity to reconnect with Missouri's prolific past.

The site of Arrow Rock and its prominent bluffs were noted on French maps of the region as early as 1732, "pierre fleche," or the "rock of arrows." Arrow Rock served as an important town for pioneers heading west on what would become the Santa Fe Trail. Those early pioneers filled their water barrels at the Big Spring, which still flows behind the Old Tavern.

Be sure to visit the Arrow Rock State Historic Site's museum for a grand introduction to Booneslick Country. The excellent visitors center here offers a movie, exhibits, hiking trails, fishing and a very spacious and secluded campground on this 167-acre site. Call (660) 837-3330.

The state has restored Arrow Rock's one-room jail, the old courthouse and the home of artist George Caleb Bingham. Bingham was a preeminent artist of the 1800s, known for his depictions of early river life, such as his famous painting *Jolly Flatboatman.*

Other stops in town include the Historic Arrow Rock Tavern, which has been serving travelers since 1834. The tavern is the oldest continuously operating restaurant west of the Mississippi River, serving food since the early days of the Santa Fe Trail. It is located on Main Street, one block from the Lyceum Theatre. Reservations requested. Mike & Mary Duncan are the proprietors. Call (660) 837-3200.

The town's Lyceum Theater is considered "Missouri's Best Theater" by readers of *Rural Missouri.* Missouri's oldest professional regional theater celebrates its 44th anniversary season in the beautifully expanded 408-seat theater. Professional actors at the award-winning theater combine their exceptional talent with the hospitality of Arrow Rock for an unforgettable experience. Visit their website for show dates. Reservations recommended. (660) 837-3311. www.lyceumtheatre.org.

Guided tours of Arrow Rock's historic buildings are available through the Friends of Arrow Rock. A choice of tours allow you to view restored structures of the mid-19th century. Tours include Huston Tavern, Bingham House, Sappington Museum and Court House, or Huston Tavern, Lodge Hall, Print Shop, Sites Gun Shop and Victorian House. Call the Friends of Arrow Rock for more information: (660) 837-3231.

(660) 837-3305 • www.arrowrock.org

Today's Trail

Explore Boone's Lick State Historic Site

Located 12 miles northwest of Boonville, Boone's Lick State Historic Site preserves a 52-acre complex that includes the salty springs, or licks, where Nathan Boone and his brother Daniel Morgan Boone began producing salt in 1805. The road to them became known as the Boone's Lick Trail and the region became known as the Boonslick area.

Salt was a crucial meat preservative for pioneers heading west. The salty water was boiled, producing about one bushel of salt for every 300 gallons of water. At its heyday, the lick employed 20 men operating two furnaces handling 60 kettles each. About 30 bushels of salt were being produced each day, then shipped to St. Louis where they sold for about $2.50 per bushel.

Today's quiet, pastoral setting belies the toil of these early laborers. A walking trail and interpretive signs talk about the area's history. Be sure to visit the Arrow Rock State Historic Site first for more comprehensive exhibits and to see relics and area artifacts from this site.

(800) 334-6946 • www.mostateparks.com/booneslick.htm

Expedition Entry
Near Lisbon Bottom
Saturday, June 9, 1804

After a heavy rain, Mother Nature tests the boat crew today. After setting out into swift waters, the crew is detained early on after hitting a log snag. After passing a prairie called "Prarie of the Arrows," near present-day Arrow Rock, the crew faces one of its defining moments on the lower Missouri River. After the stern strikes a submerged log, the current turns the boat against some drift and snags.

Clark wrote, "This was a disagreeable and Dangerous Situation, particularly as immense large trees were Drifting down and we lay imediately in their Course. Some of our men being prepared for all Situations leaped into the water Swam ashore with a roap, and fixed themselves in Such Situations, that the boat was off in a fiew minits. I can Say with Confidence that our party is not inferior to any that was ever on the waters of the Missoppie."

The river continues to rise slowly. Clark notes that the current was "excessive rapid." He writes of the delightful land to be found in this stretch. The crew makes 13 miles of progress today before setting up camp. It starts to rain again at 5 p.m. and continues throughout much of the night.

Today's Trail
Explore Lisbon Bottom

Lisbon Bottom is part of the Big Muddy National Fish & Wildlife Refuge, a series of sites between Kansas City and St. Louis that cover some 10,000 acres of bottomland. The refuge began in an effort to reopen portions of the historic floodplain to reduce future flooding and to restore habitat. The refuge hopes to eventually acquire 60,000 acres (approximately 8-percent of the floodplain). To join hikes and floats to these refuges, contact the Friends of the Big Muddy. They also coordinate river clean ups, trail-building and other events that create easier access to and enjoyment of these areas: www.friendsofbigmuddy.org.

Today's Trail

Explore Glasgow, Missouri

Glasgow, population 1,295, is probably remembered best by early rivermen for being on the tightest bend in the Missouri River. Another story goes that the town was favored by those early boat crews, who enjoyed the fragrance of its flowers from a mile away.

A Lewis & Clark historical marker is located at the riverfront. On June 10, 1804, the expedition passed the high bluff on which Glasgow would later be built, and encountered the Chariton River coming in at a hairpin bend. A few miles after passing Chicot, or Stump Island, they camped for two nights on June 10 and 11, 1804. The Captains walked through the prairie and noted the abundance of plant and animal species. The city park and river access are just east of Highway 87 at Glasgow. Call City Hall for more information: (660) 338-2377.

If you are a bookworm, check out the Lewis Library, considered by many to be the oldest library west of the Mississippi. The Glasgow Community Museum is located in the old Presbyterian Church, built in 1861. It contains exhibits on the city's history and three paintings by Glasgow artist Cornelia Kuemmel. The museum, at 4th & Commerce, is open from May 15 through October 15. Be sure to visit the old-fashioned soda fountain on Main Street, too.

Local lore has it that William Clark's name is inscribed on a fairly inaccessible bluff in this area, but I haven't had a chance to check this out yet and there is no mention of this in the journals.

Expedition Entry
Near Cambridge, Missouri
Sunday, June 10 – Monday, June 11, 1804

Clark writes that after a hard rain last night, the crew sets out very early this morning. They pass several difficult stretches of river. He notes seeing a number of goslings. The boats pass near a bank which begins to fall in as they travel by, taking many large cottonwood trees with it. The two captains walk about three miles into a "country roleing open & rich, with plenty of water, great quantities of deer." Clark writes, "I discovered a Plumb, which grows on bushes the hight of hazel, those plumbs are in great numbers, the bushes beare Verry full, about double the Sise of the wild plumb Called the Osage Plumb & am told they are finely flavoured."

The crew makes ten miles of progress today. "Our party in high Spirits," Clark writes. On June 11, due to a strong headwind, the party takes advantage of the good weather to dry out their wet articles, to examine provisions and clean their weapons. Clark notes that he has a bad cold. The river has started to fall. The hunters bring in two deer and two bear. Clark writes "men verry lively Dancing & Singing &c."

Expedition Entry
Tuesday, June 12, 1804

After passing Plumb Creek, the crew halts to eat after making nine miles. Several canoes come downriver from the Sioux nation. In the party is Pierre Dorion, an old man who has been living with the Sioux for 20 years and has great influence with them. The Corps prevails upon Dorian to return upriver with the expedition. The Captains hope to convince some of the Sioux Chiefs to return for a visit with the

President. Dorion would later escort a delegation of Yankton Chiefs to St. Louis for the Captains. The Corps purchases 300 pounds of "Voyagers Grece," most likely buffalo grease and tallow, perhaps for making pemmican. They talk with the group until late into the night, then decide to camp here.

Today's Trail
Explore Brunswick, Missouri

This river town was laid out in 1836, one mile below the mouth of the Grand River. The town's future as a shipping point dimmed as the railroad bypassed the community, and in 1875, the Missouri River changed its course and left Brunswick a mile inland on the Grand River. Today, Brunswick is known best as the center of the state's pecan-growing region, with more than 10,000 pecan trees growing in the rich river bottom soils. Brunswick is also home to the world's largest pecan, which you'll see on the side of the road. It weighs 12,000 pounds (and it happens to be made out of steel).

(660) 548-3028 • www.brunswickmo.com

Expedition Entry
Near Brunswick, Missouri
Wednesday, June 13, 1804

Clark mentions passing a round bend and two creeks called the round bend creeks. Between those creeks, he writes, "is a prarie in which the Missouries Indians once lived and the Spot where 300 of them fell a Sacrifise to the fury of the Saukees. This nation (Missouries) once the most noumerous nation in this part of the Continent, now reduced to about 80 families." According to one historian, the last full-blooded Missouri is said to have died in Oklahoma in 1907.

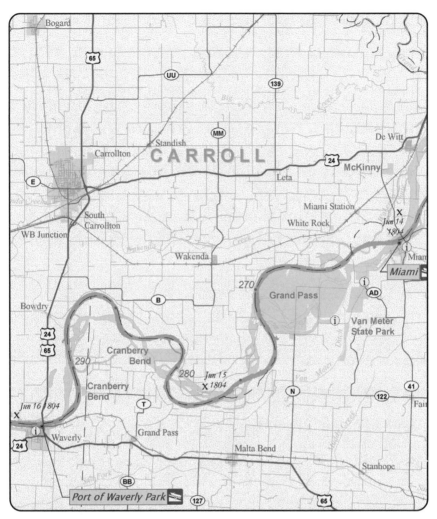

From June 14 – 16, 1804, the Corps traveled from near present-day Miami upriver to Waverly. Explore what the river looked like in the days of Lewis & Clark by visiting the 4,711-acre Grand Pass Conservation Area. A series of levees, roads and trails are great for bird watching. Habitats range from bottomland forest, wetlands and even an island.

Clark goes on to mention a sand bar collapsing with such turbulence as to nearly turn the boat over. The crew camps at the mouth of the Grand River. "This is a butifull place," Clark writes. "Took some looner observations which Kept Cap L. & my Self up untill half pass 11 oClock."

June 14, 1804

Expedition Entry
Thursday, June 14, 1804

After setting out in a thick fog, the crew faces another challenging encounter with the Mighty Mo. Clark calls it the place of snakes. "The worst place I have seen. A sand bar making out 2/3 cross the river. Sand Collecting & forming Bars and Bars washing away, the boat struck and turned, She was near oversetting. We saved her by Some extrodany exertions of our party, ever ready to inconture any fatigue for the premotion of the enterprise... we were obliged to run great rish of Loseing both Boat & men."

"G. Drewyer tels of a remarkable Snake inhabiting a small lake 5 miles below, which gobbles like a Turkey & may be herd Several miles, this Snake is of emence size," Clark writes.

Today's Trail
Explore Miami, Missouri

Miami is located on a sweeping blufftop high above the Missouri River valley. The town was platted as Greenville in 1838, then renamed to Miami in 1853. The name remembers a group of Miami Indians who established a village there around 1810. Miami, a derivative of a Chippewa word, means "People who live on the peninsula."

By 1840, Miami was an important river port, shipping large quantities of hemp and other agricultural products to markets in St. Louis. Today, be sure to visit the area restaurant and the interesting local museum or attend one of Miami's annual events, such as the Hog Dinner or 4th of July celebration.

(660) 852-3396 • www.sullivansfarms.net/friendsofmiami/

Today's Trail
Explore Van Meter State Park
Miami, Missouri

Located 12 miles northwest of Marshall, the area of Van Meter State Park was the homeland of the Missouri Indians through the early 1700s. The Missouri Indians later gave their name to the state of Missouri, as well as to the Missouri River.

Prehistoric Indian burial mounds and the "old fort," a six-acre earthwork at the site, predate the arrival of the Missouri Indians. The 983-acre park has a visitors center that features Native American presentations and year-round workshops. There is also a campground, hiking trails and a fishing lake.

(800) 334-6946 • www.mostateparks.com/vanmeter.htm

Today's Trail
Explore Grand Pass Conservation Area
Near Miami, Missouri

The 4,711-acre Grand Pass Conservation Area is a haven for waterfowl, migratory birds, shore birds, geese and ducks. A braided series of levees, roads and trails make for excellent bird watching, especially in February and March. Habitats range from bottomland forest to wetlands, and even a river island.

Expect to find migratory songbirds and nesting wood ducks in the bottomland forest. The wetlands are a popular place to see Canada geese and snow geese in the winter, and shore birds feed along the river island and mudflats in the spring.

(660) 530-5500

Expedition Entry
Friday, June 15, 1804

The crew sets out early again and have not proceeded very far before the boat wheels around on a sawyer (a sunken log), "which was near injuring us Verry much... near doeing her great damage... the river is riseing fast & the water exceedingly Swift," Clark writes. "This is said to be the worst part of the river."

He continues on, "a verry bad place, moveing sands, we were nearly being Swallowed up by the roleing Sands over which the Current was So Strong that we Could not Stem it with our Sales under a Stiff breese in addition to our ores, we were Compelled to pass under a bank which was falling in, and use our Tow rope occasionally." The expedition makes 12 and a quarter miles today.

Expedition Entry
Near Waverly, Missouri
Saturday, June 16, 1804

The crew makes ten miles progress today, despite Clark mentioning a bad sand bar "the worst I had Seen, which the boat must pass or Drop back Several Miles & Stem a Swift Current on the opsd Side of an island." Once the boat arrived there, however, it "assended the middle of the Streem which was diffucult and Dangerious. We Came to above this place at Dark and Camped in a bad place, the misquitoes and Ticks are nourmerous and bad," Clark writes.

Today's Trail
Explore Waverly, Missouri

The welcoming town of Waverly is near the expedition's campsite for June 16, 1804. And the campsites for June 17 and 18, 1804 are not much further upriver. There is an excellent restaurant, boat ramp and riverfront park here. This region is known for its picturesque apple orchards that cover many of the area's rolling hills. In addition to apple orchards, mining was long a mainstay of the area economy, employing 2,500 miners in Waverly at one time.

Expedition Entry
Sunday, June 17 & Monday, June 18, 1804

The better part of the day is spent making oars and a tow rope. Clark measures the current by floating a stick downriver and timing it. He calculates the river in the most rapid part to be traveling about 23.6 miles per hour! (Although the normal river current was generally measured at five to seven miles an hour.) Clark notes much of the party is afflicted with boils and several have dysentery. "The countery about this place is butifull," he writes. "The Ticks & Musquetors are verry troublesom."

Expedition Entry
Near Lexington, Missouri
Tuesday, June 19, 1804

After enduring rain for most of the night, the crew finishes the new oars and sets out under a gentle breeze and proceeds on past two large islands. Clark observes gooseberries and raspberries in great abundance. The crew makes 17 and a half miles progress.

Expedition Entry
Near Lexington, Missouri
Wednesday, June 20, 1804

The expedition travels almost seven miles today. "The Swet run off our men in a Stream when they row hard," Clark writes. He sees a large beautiful prairie called Sauke Prairie and pelicans on a sand bar. York nearly loses an eye after one of the men throws sand at him in fun. The crew passes a sand bar "over which the water riffleed and roered like a great fall." Clark writes, "a butifull night but the air exceedingly Damp, & the mosquiters verry troublesom." Lunar observations keep Clark up until 1 a.m.

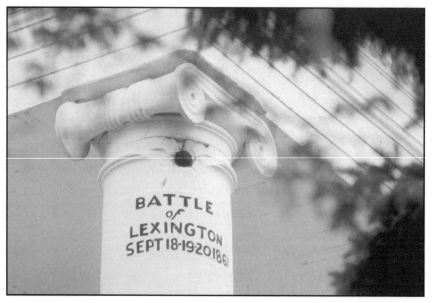

*A Civil War cannon ball is stuck in a pillar of the Lexington Courthouse.
Today, cannons have to be checked at the front desk before entering.*

Today's Trail
Explore Lexington, Missouri

Lexington, founded in 1822, was the original headquarters
of Russell, Majors & Waddell, the primary outfitters and
suppliers of goods along the Santa Fe Trail. These three men
later helped to found the Pony Express in St. Joseph, Missouri.

Today, Lexington is best known for the prestigious
Wentworth Military Academy, the more than 130 antebellum
homes located here and the Lafayette County Courthouse.

When you visit the courthouse, look for the Union Army's
Civil War cannonball still visibly wedged into the top of the
structure's column (having missed General Sterling Price's
headquarters across the street, when originally fired September
of 1861). Today a variety of antique shops and bed & breakfasts
make this a popular weekend getaway from Kansas City.

(660) 259-4711 • www.historiclexington.com

Today's Trail

Explore the Battle of Lexington State Historic Site
Lexington, Missouri

Explore this Civil War battlefield that preserves the remnants of the original trenches and the graves of unknown Union troops on this 100-acre site. Tour the 1853 Anderson House, once called "the largest and best arranged dwelling house west of St. Louis." The home is better known for the three days of strife that occurred here in 1861, when it was a fiercely contested prize in a battle between the Union Army and the Missouri State Guard. A visitors center explains the events of September 1861, and why the "Battle of the Hemp Bales" lifted Southern spirits and dampened the North's hopes of an easy victory in the struggle to control Missouri. The spirits of several soldiers are said to still linger here.

(800) 334-6946
www.mostateparks.com/lexington/lexington.htm

Tour the 1853 Anderson House, once called "the largest and best arranged dwelling house west of St. Louis." This house was home to a bloody three-day battle during the Civil War.

Region Review

From Lexington to Kansas City, Missouri

June 20 – 25, 1804

On the stretch of river from Lexington to Kansas City, howling winds, stretches of roaring river, mosquitos and rain continue to challenge the Corps as they work their way slowly up the Missouri River, averaging half a dozen or so miles of progress a day.

Clark writes of "butifull" prairie almost daily, and notes abundant berries and game. Today, this stretch of river offers secluded, sleepy river hamlets, the must–visit Fort Osage and numerous Lewis & Clark related sites worth visiting in Kansas City.

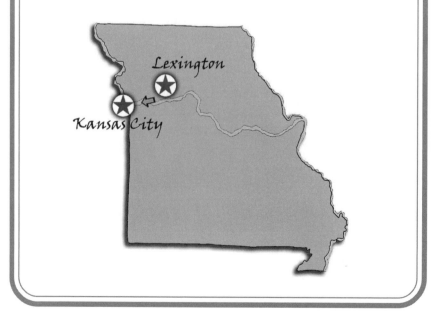

Today's Trail
Explore Wellington, Missouri

Once a village best known for coal-mining, this town's name was probably chosen to remember the Duke of Wellington, who defeated Napoleon at Waterloo. The towns of Napoleon and Waterloo are also located nearby.

Expedition Entry
Near Wellington, Missouri
Thursday, June 21, 1804

The river has risen three inches in the night. Today, the crew is faced with the task of getting the boats past the "roering" waters noted in yesterday's entry. Pierre Cruzatte examines a small island for the best route around it. Clark writes, "The water on each Side of the Island presented a most unfavourable prospect of Swift water over roleing Sands which rored like an immence falls." The crew sets out, determined to ascend on the north side, sometimes rowing, poling and drawing up with a strong rope. Clark writes, "we assended without wheeling or receiving any damige more than breakeing one of my starboard Windows, and looseing Some oars which were Swong under the windows."

Also in today's journal, Clark offers an answer to whether the Big Muddy has always been, as Mark Twain put it, "too thick to drink, too thin to plow." Clark writes, "The water we Drink, or the Common water of the missourie at this time, contains half a Comn Wine Glass of ooze or mud to every pint."

Clark writes that the bottomlands are covered with cottonwood and willows "subject to overflow," with rich, fertile soils in the high bottoms, filled with cottonwood, walnut, ash, hackberry, mulberry, linden and sycamore in great abundance just out of the riverbottoms.

A classic Missouri sunset rewards the crew for their exertions in getting the boats upriver seven miles today. Clark writes, "at Sun Set the atmespier presented every appearance of wind, Blue & white Streeks Centering at the Sun as She disappeared and the Clouds Situated to the S.W., Guilde in the most butifull manner."

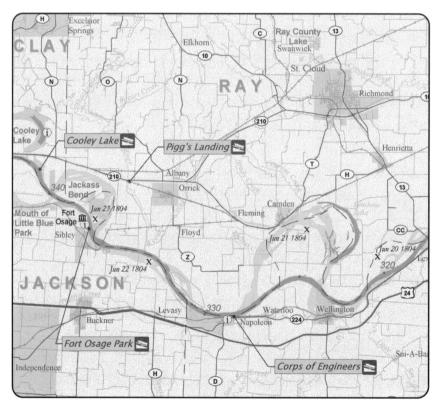

Be sure to visit the reconstructed log fort at Fort Osage, the site of the expedition's camp on June 23, 1804. Note how the Corps of Discovery's June 21, 1804 camp is now located far from the river. The faint outline of the river's previous course is an example of an oxbow lake that, through channelization by the Corps of Engineers, is no longer connected to the main channel.

Today's Trail
Explore Waterloo, Missouri

Waterloo was coined the "City of the Classic Fox," due to its proximity to the Fox River. Tradition says that a Frenchman who fought in Napoleon's army lived here. Another source says the town was named because of its nearby water source. Once a coal-mining village, the town was the county seat from 1836 to 1846, and again from 1854 to 1865. Each time it experienced growth. However, the town declined when the county seat moved to Kahoka.

Today's Trail
Explore Napoleon, Missouri

This small river town was established in 1836 and called Poston's Landing after a storekeeper. Its name later changed to Lisbon, after the mayor's daughter. But, like many other towns, the post office name was already chosen, and the town changed its name to Napoleon. The name is particularly appropriate for a town in Lafayette County, a county named after a French general. A popular local saying of the nearby towns of Waterloo and Wellington is "Napoleon and Wellington met at Waterloo."

Expedition Entry
Near Levasy, Missouri
Friday, June 22, 1804

The river rises another four inches during the night. Clark is awakened before daylight by the guard preparing the boat for an impending storm. At dawn, violent winds and rain come from the west and last for about an hour. It clears away, and the Corps "set out and proceeded on under a gentle breeze" from the northwest. They pass some very swift water crowded with snags, two large islands opposite of each other and a large and extensive "butifull" prairie on the larboard side.

June 23, 1804

Captain Lewis walks on shore for a few miles this afternoon. After reaching the mouth of a large creek called the River of the Fire Prairie, the boat crews reunite with a party of hunters, who inform them that the lands they have just traveled through are fine and well watered.

Expedition Entry
Near Sibley, Missouri
Saturday, June 23, 1804

The river drops eight inches during the night. The crew proceeds on at 7 a.m. A hard wind blowing downriver prevents the party from moving from an island the whole day. Captain Lewis examines the artillery. At the lower end of the island, Clark gets out of the boat to walk on shore, expecting the party to reach him later in the day. He proceeds around an extensive bend in the river, kills a deer and makes a fire, expecting the boat to come upriver in the evening. The continued winds prevent the boats from making any progress.

"As the distance by land was too great for me to return by night, I concluded to Camp, Peeled Some bark to lay on, and geathered wood to make fires to Keep off the musquitor & Knats. Heard the party on Shore fire, at Dark, Drewyer came to me with the horses, one fat bear & a deer," he writes.

Today's Trail
Explore Sibley, Missouri

Today the small community of Sibley acts as a gateway to Fort Osage, which was originally called Fort Clark. The town is named for George Sibley, who commanded Fort Osage from 1818 through 1826.

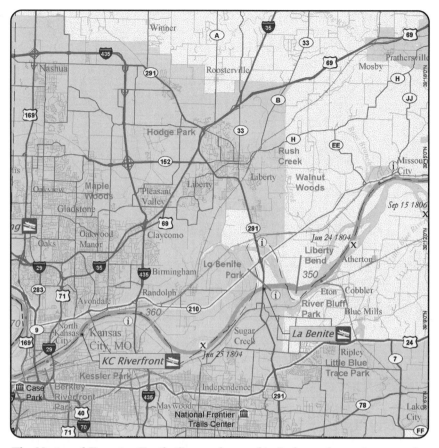

The National Frontier Trails Center, located in Independence, is a popular stop for history trekkers. It is located a short drive away from the river and the expedition's June 25, 1804 camp. For more information, call: (816) 325-7575. Online at www.frontiertrailscenter.com.

Today's Trail

Explore Fort Osage National Historic Landmark
Sibley, Missouri

Fort Osage was the second U.S. outpost built in the Louisiana Purchase. The site, overlooking a wide stretch of the Missouri, was first noted as a promising fort location by Clark on the Corps' return trip in 1806. Clark returned to this site in 1808 with Captain Clemson and soldiers to erect a fort. It served several functions. It was a trade house to sell and trade with area Native Americans, it was an outpost in the new territory and it also served as a sanctuary for Missouri's first settlers. It remained the westernmost U.S. government presence until 1818. During its 19 years of existence, Fort Osage hosted explorers, dignitaries, trappers, traders and the great Native American leaders. Due to lobbying from the private sector, who resented the governmental competition and since the frontier had pushed further westward, the fort closed its doors in 1827. Today you can actually explore many of the reconstructed fort's buildings, which are maintained by Jackson County Parks and

Recreation. Today's fort is built upon the original footings using the fort plans still in existence in Washington, D.C. Visit the blockhouses, barracks, blacksmith shop, interpreter's cabin and trade house. Fort Osage's museum details early military uniforms, and the gift shop is one of the trail's best. Watch the museum's video, and check out the ancient dugout canoe displayed inside. Be sure to hear the story about how it was discovered. Events throughout the year transport you back to the 1800s. The Discovery Expedition of St. Charles plans to camp at Fort Osage from June 23 to 28, 2004.

(816) 795-8200 • www.historicfortosage.com

June 24, 1804

Expedition Entry
Near Atherton, Missouri
Sunday, June 24, 1804

Clark writes in more detail about his brief adventure away from the boats. "I joined the Boat theis morning with a fat Bear & two Deer, last enining I Struck the river about 6 miles (by land) abov the Boat, and finding it too late to get to the Boat, and the wind blowing So hard Down the river that She could not assend, I concluded to Camp, altho I had nothing but my hunting Dress, & the Musquitors Ticks & Knats verry troublesom, I concluded to hunt on a Willow Island Situated close under the Shore, in Crossing from an Island, I got mired, and was obliged to Craul out, a disagreeable Situation & a Diverting one of any one who Could have Seen me after I got out, all Covered with mud, I went my Camp & scraped off the Mud and washed my Clothes, and fired off my gun which was answered by George Drewyer who was in persute of me & campe up at Dark. We feasted of meet & water, the latter we made great use of being much fatigued & thirsty."

Clark notes "emince number of Deer on both Sides of the river," and "great quantites of Bear Sign, they are after Mulbiries which are in great quantities." Lewis walks on shore and kills a deer today. Drewyer kills two, with Fields also killing one.

The boats pass between two sandbars at the head of which the crew had to raise the keelboat eight inches to get her over. After making a total of 11 and a half miles of progress today, the crew camps at the lower point of an island on the starboard side. The party is in high spirits.

Today's Trail
Visit River Bluff Park
Kansas City, Missouri

River Bluff Park is located at Liberty Bend, a treacherous bend in the river that was eliminated by the Corps of Engineers. They dug a canal one mile long to cut off five miles of river and actually constructed a bridge on dry land, then dug a canal under it.

Expedition Entry
Near Kansas City, Missouri
Monday, June 25, 1804

During the night, the river falls another eight inches. A thick fog detains the crew for an hour before they are able to embark. Clark notes a coal bank on the larboard side, which "appears to Contain a great quantity of excellente Coal." The crew passes a small creek on the larboard side called Bennet's Creek. "The Prairies Come within a Short distance of the river on each Side which Contains in addition to Plumbs, Raspberries & vast quantities of wild crab apples and wildflowers. Great numbers of deer are seen feeding on the young willows." The hunters and shore party do not rejoin the boat crew this evening. The boat crew camps on an island. The river is still falling fast.

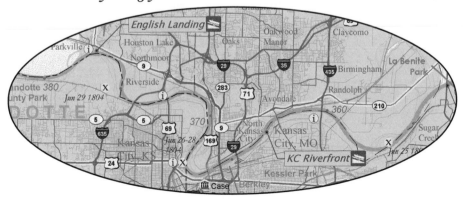

Another look at Fort Osage, which overlooks a wide stretch of the Missouri. Clark returned to this site in 1808 to oversee the fort's construction.

Region Review
From Kansas City to St. Joseph & Beyond...

June 26 – July 18, 1804

*I*n this last installment of Clark's journals from 1804 while the Corps was still in present-day Missouri, the Corps travels 180 miles from the site of present-day Kansas City to the northwest corner of the state.

At present-day Little Bean Marsh Conservation Area in Missouri, the crew "ussered in the day by a discharge of one shot from our Bow piece," in celebration of the Fourth of July—considered the westernmost official observance of Independence Day in the newly acquired Louisiana Purchase territory. The Fourth of July would be celebrated in present-day Kansas before the day was out as well.

After traveling almost 600 miles up the Missouri River, the expedition leaves the present-day state of Missouri on July 18, 1804 and heads onward, further upriver, to explore the present-day states of Nebraska and Iowa.

Seemingly limitless prairies remind the explorers of farms back home, while abundant deer keeps them well fed, with additional sightings of elk and buffalo tantalizing the hunters.

Ancient graves remind the explorers that they are not the first to set foot here. A thunderstorm threatens their progress. And throughout their entries, the term "butifull" remains their favorite word.

York and Lewis' dog Seaman are prominently featured along with Sacagawea, Lewis and Clark in a towering bronze statue at Kansas City's Case Park (shown above and on opposite page). This park offers an excellent view of the confluence of the Missouri and Kaw Rivers.

Today's Trail

Explore Kansas City, Missouri

High above the confluence of the Missouri and Kaw Rivers, Case Park offers a unique vantage point from which to view much of the Kansas City area. This location was noted by Clark on June 28, 1804. On their return trip, Lewis & Clark both scaled this hill on September 15, 1806. In his journal entry (see page 229), Clark wrote of passing the mouth of the Kaw (also known as the Kansas) River...

About a mile below we landed and Capt Lewis and my Self assended a hill which appeared to have a Commanding Situation for a fort, the Shore is bold and rocky immediately at the foot of the hill, from the top of the hill you have a perfect Command of the river, this hill fronts the Kanzas and has a view of the Missouri a Short distance above that river...

Today, you can enjoy the view the captain's shared on that day in 1806. A bronze of Lewis, Clark, York, Sacagawea and their dog Seaman is located in the center of this park.

*The Kansas City Riverfront Park offers nice views of the
Missouri River and easy access to an 18-mile pedestrian
and bicycle trail called the Riverfront Heritage Trail.*

Kansas City will take part in a bi-state bicentennial
signature event to be celebrated collectively by Kansas City,
Missouri, and in Kansas by both Atchison and Leavenworth. The
event is to commemorate the first Independence Day observance
in the newly formed Louisiana Territory. The 2004 event will
include an extensive list of activities lasting nearly three weeks,
June 19 – July 11, 2004. (800) 858-1749. www.journey4th.org.

Even long before pioneers came through the area, this land
was inhabited by the Osage, Kansas and Wyandotte. In the late
1700s and early 1800s, trappers and traders began to develop
the town of Kansas (later to be called Kansas City) on the
southern bank of the Missouri River, a short distance from the
confluence with the Kansas, or Kaw, River. The town's location
on the banks of the Missouri River made K.C. an important
gateway town for pioneers traveling west along the Oregon,
Santa Fe and California Trails. Other area highlights for Lewis
& Clark aficionados include the National Frontier Trails Center
in Independence, Powell Gardens and Westport's Pioneer Park.

(816) 325-7575 • www.frontiertrailscenter.com
(816) 697-2600 • www.powellgardens.org

Today's Trail

Explore the Steamboat Arabia Museum
Kansas City, Missouri

The hardest thing about writing guidebooks is briefly mentioning stops along the trail that deserve entire chapters. The Steamboat Arabia Museum is just such a place. Nowhere else does pioneer life and early river travel come to life more vividly than at this wonderful museum. You will be amazed at the story of this treasure-hunting family, who excavated the Steamboat Arabia 132 years after it sank in the Missouri River in 1856. Within minutes of hitting a huge snag, much of the boat and virtually all 222 tons of precious frontier cargo lay at the bottom of the Missouri River. The Arabia went down so fast, that the cargo bound for frontier stores was still all intact. The swirling current soon engulfed the boat, eventually covering it with a fine silt, which remarkably preserved the boat's contents.Today, those items have been cleaned and are on display along with the original paddlewheel and the story of the unfortunate mule that someone forget to untie. Located at 400 Grand Boulevard at the Kansas City River Market.

(816) 471-1856 • www.1856.com

Today's Trail

Explore the Kansas City River Market
Kansas City, Missouri

Pioneers have disembarked at Kansas City's River Market since the steamboat days to begin their overland adventure out west. The River Market area was bustling with the comings and goings of a young country determined to make a better life out of the seemingly limitless wilderness. Although today's River Market denizens are more likely to arrive in air-conditioned SUVs, the spirit of the market is the same: enjoy the hustle and bustle of the city's soul, discover a treasure for your house, squeeze some melons and, if you're lucky, hear "Almost Willy" belt out a ballad (upper photo, opposite page).

The first market house was constructed here in 1858, which has been the site of the City Market ever since. Missouri's largest open-air farmers market not only offers fresh produce, flowers and herbs, but more exotic fruits and vegetables given the city's diverse inhabitants. You'll also find antique shops, restaurants, art galleries and the Steamboat Arabia Museum (see previous page).

If you're visiting mid-week, visit the River Market's Organic Market on Wednesday nights from 4 to 8 p.m. through October. Enjoy fresh vegetables, flowers and live music.
www.kc-citymarket.com
(816) 471-6789 • www.kansascityrivermarket.com

Today's Trail
Explore the Conservation Department's Discovery Center
Kansas City, Missouri

Be sure to visit the Discovery Center at the Country Club Plaza—an urban interpretive center of the Missouri Department of Conservation, replete with a wonderful Michael Haynes panoramic Lewis & Clark mural (see his work at www.mhaynesart.com), a Lewis & Clark movie, a scaled-down keelboat and a full calendar of events. 4750 Troost Avenue.

(816) 759-7300

www.conservation.state.mo.us/areas/kcmetro/discovery

Expedition Entry

At present-day Kansas City, Missouri
Tuesday, June 26, 1804

The crew sets out early. The river has fallen a little, with winds from the southwest. The crew passes the mouth of Blue Water River (in French, Riviere La Bleue, now known as the Big Blue or Blue River) on the larboard side.

Not much further upriver, Clark writes, "the river appears to be Confd. In a verry narrow Channel, and the Current Still more So by Couenter Current or Whirl on one Side & high bank on the other... we Killed a large rattle Snake, Sunning himself in the bank... passed a bad Sand bar, where our tow rope broke twice, & with great exertions we rowed round it and Came to & Camped in the Point above the Kansas River. I observed a great number of Parrot queets this evening, our Party Killed... 7 Deer to day."

This is the first mention of the Carolina parakeet west of the Mississippi. The bird is now extinct.

Expedition Entry

Wednesday, June 27, 1804

Lewis makes observations at the confluence of the "Kancez River" and the Mighty Missouri. Clark writes that the day starts fair and warm. He writes, "we determin to delay at this Place three or four Days to make observations & recruit the party. Several men out Hunting, unloaded one Perogue, and turned her up to Dry with a view of repairing her after Completeing a Strong redoubt or best work frome one river to the other, of logs & Bushes Six feet high."

June 28, 1804

Clark writes that the country about the mouth of the Kansas River is very fine. He notes the Kansas River is 230 yards wide and the Missouri River at this point is about 500 yards wide.

Expedition Entry
Thursday, June 28, 1804

Today, the pirogue is repaired and the boats are cleaned out. The provisions of the boats are examined and laid out to dry. Clark notes, "in examineing our private Store of Provisions we found Several articles Spoiled from the wet or dampness they had received." Eight to ten hunters go out in various directions. The river has risen two feet since the previous evening. Clark notes that the hunters killed several deer and saw buffalo. Of the site at the confluence, Clark writes, "a butifull place for a fort, good landing place, the waters of the Kansas verry disigreeably tasted to me."

Regarding the Kansas River, Clark writes, "This River recvies its name from a nation which dwells at this time on its banks & 2 villages one about 20 Leagues & the other 40 Leagues up, those Indians are not verry nourmerous at this time, reduced by war with their neighbours, &c. they formerly liveid on the South banks of the Missouries 24 Leagues above this river in a open & butifull plain and were verry numerous at the time the french first Settled the Illinois, I am told they are a fierce & warlike people, being badly Supplied with fire arms, become easily conquered by the Aiauway & Saukees who are better furnished with those materials of war, This nation is now out in the plains hunting the Buffalow."

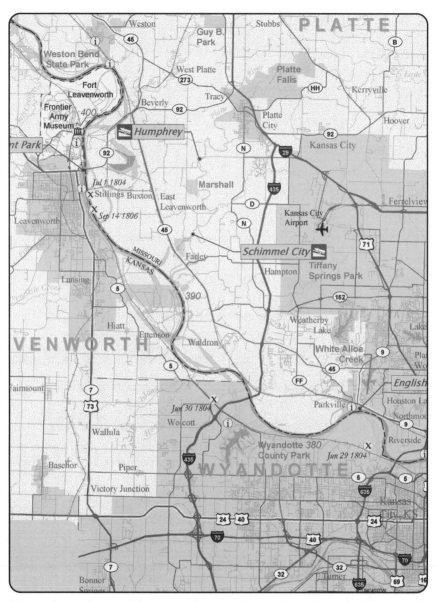

Stops along the trail between Kansas City and St. Joseph offer a wide variety of options: walk a shaded riverfront trail at Parkville, tour a Harley plant, visit the Military Museum in St. Joe, or visit the Buffalo Soldiers monument at Fort Leavenworth. Lewis & Clark trekkers will enjoy the riverviews at Parkville, St. Joe's Wyeth Park and Weston Bend State Park.

June 29, 1804

Expedition Entry
Near Riverside, Missouri
Friday, June 29, 1804

The crew remains at camp until 4:30 p.m. to hold a court martial. Crewmember John Collins is charged with "getting drunk on his post this morning out of whiskey put under his Charge as a Sentinal and for Suffering Hugh Hall to draw whiskey out of the Said Barrel intended for the party." Both Collins and Hall are found guilty. Punishment was 100 lashes on his bare back for Collins (who was on guard duty at the time), and 50 lashes for Hall. The crew then resume their travel upriver, making a little over seven miles today.

The Mighty Mo once again tests the crew, as they barely escape yet another accident that could have stopped the expedition in its tracks. Clark writes, "Passed a verry bad place of water, the Sturn of the Boat Struck a moveing Sand & turned within 6 inches of a large Sawyer (underwater log), if the Boat had Struck the Sawyer, her Bow must have been Knocked off & in Course She must hav Sunk in the Deep water below." In his second journal, Clark added, "the rapidity with which the Boat turned was so great that if her bow had Struck the Snag, She must have either turned over or the bow nocked off."

Today's Trail

Explore Parkville, Missouri

Parkville's English Landing Park is a welcoming riverfront park full of flat, paved, shaded walking trails with excellent river views and numerous picnic shelters. Just steps away, Parkville's well-kept historic riverfront business district offers a variety of antiquing, shopping and dining options, as well as a weekly farmers market. Be sure to explore the nearby Parkville Nature Sanctuary. Trail maps are available at the main entrance, just below City Hall. Check out City Hall's arrowhead exhibit, and drive the underground loop at Parkville University for the kids. From May through October, Saturday mornings and Wednesday evenings coming alive with visitors wandering through Parkville's Farmer's Market selecting fresh produce, plants, flowers and baked goods.

(816) 741-7676 • www.parkvillemo.com

I'm sure if Lewis & Clark were to do it all over again, they'd be riding hogs. Visit the gift shop or arrange a tour (by reservation only) of the Harley-Davidson assembly plant at 11401 N. Congress. (816) 270-8488.

June 30, 1804

Expedition Entry
Saturday, June 30, 1804

The Corps of Discovery makes ten miles progress upriver today. After setting out very early, Clark sees a very large wolf on a sand bar walking near a gang of turkeys. At ten miles above the Kansas River, the crew passes the mouth of a small river called the "Petite Plate" or the "little Shole river" (today's Platte or Little Platte River). Clark writes that the small river has several "rapids & falls, well calculated for mills."

And he writes of eating some bread and bacon supplied by an unnamed party. The hunters kill nine deer today, including two bucks swimming in the river. Clark writes "Deer to be Seen in every direction and their tracks are as plenty as Hogs about a farm," and "Deer on the banks, Skipping in every derection." The crew camps on the larboard side opposite the lower point of Diamond Island.

Clark finishes the day's log with three heart-wrenching words: "Broke our mast."

April Geyman uses driftwood from the Missouri River, as well as other found materials in her folk art. See her work at the River Gallery in Leavenworth, Kansas.

Expedition Entry
Near Leavenworth, Kansas
Sunday, July 1, 1804

The month of July starts abruptly, when, in the middle of the night, one of the soldiers on patrol sounds an alarm after being "challenged" by either a man or a beast, which runs off after all of the men were "prepared for action." Clark notes passing a sand bar covered for a mile with driftwood.

The crew stops for a three-hour break due to excessive heat. Pecan trees are noted, as are great quantities of raspberries and grapes. Clark writes, "pass a run on the larboard side a butifull extensive Prarie, Two Islands just above Called Isles des Parques... one of the french hands Says 'that the french Kept their Cattle & horses on those Islands at the time they had in this quarter a fort & trading establishment.'" Clark also writes, "Mr Mackey Says the first village of the Kanseis was a little above this Island... no trace of anything of that Kind remains to be seen." The Corps makes 13 miles of progress today.

Today's Trail
Explore Leavenworth, Kansas

Be sure to browse River Gallery at 207 Delaware in Leavenworth. This place is incredible. Owner John Graham displays the unique work of more than 50 area artists, many of whom draw their inspiration or raw materials from the river environment. Some of my favorites: April Geyman's driftwood crosses, Diana Harrison's pine needle baskets and Matt Nowack's writing pens made from wood recycled from historic sites. (913) 682-7444. www.firstcityart.com.

Be sure to visit historic Fort Leavenworth, its Buffalo Soldier Monument and its Frontier Army Museum, which exhibits material culture of Frontier Army soldiers who served west of the Mississippi River between 1804 and 1917. Call (913) 684-3191.

Leavenworth's riverfront walk at First Street and Esplanade is worth exploring. Kiosks play recorded history at the touch of a button all along the route. Subjects include the history of the river, Lewis & Clark, steamboat days and more.

Expedition Entry
Near Weston, Missouri
Monday, July 2, 1804

The crew sets out early this morning, passing on the left of the "Isles des parques." The river then all at once becomes crowded with drift, making it extremely dangerous to cross. Clark supposes this sudden change is due to the caving in of the banks at the head of an island upriver. The Corps passes Turkey Creek, then passes "a verry bad Sand bar on the larboard side. The 20 Oars & Poals could with much dificuelty Stem the Current, passed a large Island on the starboard side Called by the Inds. Bear Medison Island."

At noon, the crew stops at the island. In excessive heat, they spend four hours making a mast out of a cottonwood tree, which Clark notes turned a beautiful red in the course of a day and a night. Clark writes, "Deer Sign has become So Common it is hardly necessary to mention them." The crew camps opposite the "1st old Village of the Kanzas," where the French formerly had a fort to protect the trade of this nation. The Fort de Cavagnial, named after the French governor of Louisiana, was founded in 1744 and abandoned in 1764, when Louisiana was transferred from France to Spain. It was built to control trade with the Kansa and Osage Indians.

Readers of Midwest Living Magazine *voted Weston
one of the top ten antiquing towns in the Midwest.*

*Historians in your group will love visiting Weston for its Lewis & Clark
campsite marker and its unique history. Others will enjoy the great
dining, antiques and gift shops. Be sure to stop at O'Malley's 1842
Irish Pub, in the cellars at the corner of Short and Welt Streets.*

Today's Trail
Explore Weston, Missouri

The proximity of the Missouri River and the area's rich soil attracted many Indian tribes, including the Kansa, Iowa, Sac and Fox. In the 1840s and 1850s, Weston surpassed both Kansas City and St. Joseph in size, due to Weston's burgeoning river port and bountiful tobacco crops. By 1858, Weston was recognized as the largest hemp port in the world, and it continued to be a major transportation link by land and water. Today, agriculture, including tobacco production, still plays an important role in the area's economy. Approximately seven million pounds of tobacco are sold in Platte County each year.

This small river town is also a popular daytrip destination. The well-preserved antebellum homes, winery, museums and the only tobacco auction west of the Mississippi River serve as a draw for the visitors who also savor the area bed & breakfasts, dining and shopping options. Readers of *Midwest Living Magazine* voted Weston one of the top ten antiquing towns in the Midwest. Nearby is the McCormick Distillery (not open for tours), which began operation in 1858. It is said to be the oldest continuously operating distillery in the United States.

(888) 635-7457 • http://ci.weston.mo.us

Today's Trail
Explore Weston Bend State Park
Near Weston, Missouri

Enjoy the high vantage point of this state park's Missouri River overlook. This easily accessible spot offers one of the most expansive views of the Missouri River in the entire state, including wild bottomland forests and views that stretch for almost ten miles into Kansas, on the opposite side of the river.

Take your time exploring this 1,133-acre park. One trail meanders through the woods and along the bluff, offering scenic views of the river similar to those seen by Lewis & Clark. A three-mile paved loop allows cyclists the chance to follow a creek through forests of cottonwood, sycamore and maple trees.

Signs at five old tobacco barns tell the story of the area's early tobacco trade. A playground, shelters and campsites are available.

(800) 334-6946 • www.mostateparks.com/westonbend.htm

Expedition Entry
Atchison, Kansas
Wednesday, July 4, 1804

At present-day Little Bean Marsh Conservation Area in Missouri, the crew "ussered in the day by a discharge of one shot from our Bow piece," in celebration of the Fourth of July—considered the westernmost official observance of Independence Day in the newly acquired Louisiana Purchase territory. The Fourth of July would be celebrated in present-day Kansas (near Atchison) before the day was out as well.

Later in the day, Joe Fields is bitten by a snake, which Lewis quickly doctors with bark. Clark writes, "passed a Creek... comeing out of an extensive Prarie reching within 200 yards of the river, as this Creek has no name, and this being... the 4th of July the day of independence of the U.S., [I] call it 4th of July 1804 Creek..." Clark writes, "Saw great numbers of Goslings to day which Were nearly grown, the... Lake is clear and Contain great quantities of fish an Gees & Goslings, The great quantity of those fowl... induce me to Call it Gosling Lake."

Clark also writes, "The Plains of this countrey are covered with a Leek Green Grass, well calculated for the sweetest and most norushing hay, interspersed with... trees, Spreding ther lofty branchs over Pools Springs or Brooks of fine water... Shrubs covered with the most delicious froot is to be seen in every direction, and nature appears to have exerted herself to butify the Senery by the variety of flours raiseing Delicately and highly... above the Grass, which Strikes & profumes the Sensation, and amuses the mind throws it into Conjecturing the cause of So magnificent a Senerey... in a Country thus Situated far removed from the Sivilised world to be enjoyed by nothing but the Buffalo Elk Deer & Bear in which it abounds." The crew travels 15 miles upriver today. They close the day with another discharge from the bow piece and an extra gill of whiskey for each man.

Today's Trail
Explore Atchison, Kansas

Atchison is the site of the expedition's Fourth of July celebration in 1804 (see opposite page). Call the chamber office for a complete schedule of events in 2004. In 1804, Clark named two creeks here to mark the occasion: Fourth of July 1804 Creek, located in the heart of town, and Independence Creek, located four miles north of town—closer to their camp.

The world's most famous aviatrix, Amelia Earhart, was born here at her grandparent's home on July 24, 1897. Tour that home, now the Earhart Birthplace Museum, located high above the Missouri River. Learn more about here at numerous Earhart sites and attractions, including an annual festival in July. When you arrive by river, the castle-like Benedictine Monastery high on the bluffs will astound you.

(800) 234-1854 • www.atchisonkansas.net

The Fourth of July 1804 Creek, named by Clark, is located at the intersection of Highways 59 and 73. Interpretive markers tell the story.

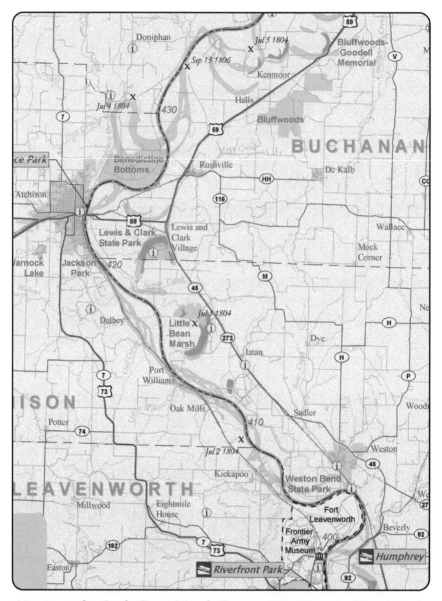

At present-day Little Bean Marsh Conservation Area in Missouri, the crew "ussered in the day by a discharge of one shot from our Bow piece," in celebration of the Fourth of July—considered the westernmost official observance of Independence Day in the newly acquired Louisiana Purchase territory.

Expedition Entry
Near Atchison, Kansas
Thursday, July 5, 1804

The crew sets out very early, passing the site of an old Kansas village, "the Cause of those people moveing from this place I cannot learn, but naterally conclude that War has reduced their nation & compelled them to retire further into the Plains with a view of defending themselves & opposeing their enemey more effectually on hors back."

Later in the day, the crew passes some very dangerous sand bars, where the crew loses control of the boat, which "turned twice on the quick Sand & once on a raft of Drift, no procievable damage." On the banks, Clark observes great quantities of summer and fall grapes, berries and wild roses. "Deer is not So plenty in this three days past as they were below that... great Deel of Elk Sign... Some Buffalo Sign." The Corps makes ten miles of progress today.

Today's Trail
Explore Lewis & Clark State Park
Near St. Joseph, Missouri

The lake that Clark described as containing "great quantities of fish and Gees & Goslings," on the Fourth of July in 1804 is known today as Lewis and Clark Lake. The Lewis and Clark State Park borders this lake. And just as Clark noted, waterfowl still flock to this oxbow lake, including geese, great blue herons, snowy egrets and ducks. A scale replica of the keelboat is located here, along with a series of interpretation signs pertaining to the expedition. A swimming beach, shady picnic spots, a playground and camping areas are also located here.

(800) 334-6946 • www.mostateparks.com/lewisandclark.htm

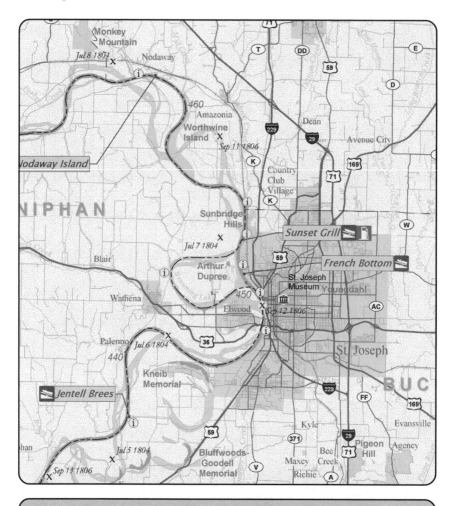

Names To Know
Joseph Robidoux

Joseph Robidoux (pronounced ROO-bi-do) is considered the founder of St. Joseph. He was the leader of a French-Canadian fur trading family that sent men out to trade with the Indians along the Missouri River and as far west as today's Wyoming, Colorado and New Mexico. Before he died in 1868, he saw his town grow to about 19,000 citizens.

St. Joe's Wyeth Park offers a spectacular view of the Missouri River—a great place to enjoy your picnic lunch while you plan your next stop. An interpretive sign here describes the expedition's crew members, whose number varied as the trip progressed. When the group passed this area in July of 1804, it consisted of 50 men, four horses and a dog.

July 6, 1804

Expedition Entry
Near St. Joseph, Missouri
Friday, July 6, 1804

"*We Set out early this morning & Proceeded on,*" *making a total of 12 miles of progress upriver today. The river is falling slowly. A very warm day.*

Observing the exertions of his crew, Clark writes, "[it is] worthy of remark that the water of this river or Some other Cause... throws out a greater [perspiration] of Swet than I could Suppose Could pass thro the humane body. Those men that do not work at all will wet a Shirt in a Few minits & those who work, the Swet will run off in Streams." The crew passes Reeveys Prairie, where the river is confined into a "verry narrow Space Crowded on the starboard side by Sands which were moveing and difficuelt to pass."

Expedition Entry
Saturday, July 7, 1804

After setting out early, the boats pass through some swift waters, "which obliged us to draw up by roapes," Clark writes. The crew passes a beautiful prairie, called St. Michul, "those Praries on the river has verry much the appearance of old farms from the river. Divided by narrow Strips of woodland," Clark writes.

A hunter kills a wolf. One crewmember (Frazer) becomes very sick, possibly due to sun stroke, which Captain Lewis treats by bleeding him and giving him "niter"—saltpeter. After progressing 14 miles today, the crew camps a short distance upriver from the area that would become St. Joseph, Missouri.

The view from Sunset Grill can't be beat. Have a seat and watch the original Nature Channel unfold with no commercial interruptions.

Today's Trail

Explore St. Joseph, Missouri

A trip to St. Joseph is like a journey straight into history. "St. Joe," is where the Pony Express began and where Jesse James met his demise. Although Missouri had become the 24th U.S. state in 1821, this area remained Indian Territory until 1837, when the federal government bargained with the Indians for 2 million acres of land. It was called the Platte Purchase and it added six northwestern counties to Missouri, among them Buchanan County, which encompasses St. Joseph. The Indians received $7,500 and "other considerations," including a 400-acre reservation across the river in the state of Kansas.

Popular St. Joseph stops include the Pony Express Museum, the Patee House Museum, the Jesse James Home, the Robidoux Row Museum, the National Military Heritage Museum and the Albrecht-Kemper Museum of Art.

Lewis & Clark aficionados should plan to spend a few full days in St. Joe. There's a lot to see. Be sure to visit the St. Joseph

Alan Carr checks out the sharp claws of a towering grizzly bear at the St. Joseph Museum.

Museum. The museum's Native American exhibits are incredible. The intricate beadwork and textiles will leave you in awe. The towering grizzly helps put the trail's early dangers in perspective: (816) 232-8471. www.stjosephmuseum.org.

The Glore Psychiatric Museum is another must-see. Have you heard of Rush's Thunderbolts? Lewis spent three months in Philadelphia before the expedition learning basic health care from Dr. Benjamin Rush, a leading physician of the day. Dr. Rush claimed his pills cured a surprisingly wide array of ailments that the expedition might encounter. Here you'll learn more about the Rush's Thunderbolts in the museum's exhibit "Medical Aspects of the Lewis & Clark Expedition." Journal

entries, documents and period artifacts illustrate the medical
challenges the Corps faced on their expedition. But perhaps
more memorable will be the museum's more esoteric displays of
the "tools of the trade" that chronicle the history of mental
health care, such as electric shock, cages and human-sized
"gerbil wheels" used to calm hyperactive patients.

St. Joe's new riverwalk is also worth exploring. It includes
some wonderful Lewis & Clark signage. Also near the riverfront
is Cordonnier's Place, at 2221 S. 4th Street. (816) 279-0826.
It's a funky little diner that's been serving locals for 25 years. A
photograph on the wall shows George Cordonnier's dad, a
riverboat captain, on an old pile-driver barge. David Cordonnier
is an avid hunter and taxidermist, who has an impressive
display of mounted deer throughout the restaurant, including
several 15-point bucks. Cordonnier's catches their own carp out
on the river and they serve it deep fried. Since catfish is
prohibited from being fished commercially, they serve deep
fried catfish that are farm raised.

Everyone will probably turn to look at you when you come
in, but if you don't mind saying hello first, you're sure to find
some fellow river rats here that can really tell you some stories.
Start out by asking why there's a chunk of Missouri on the
Kansas side of the Missouri River (the airport). It was also here
that I heard the story about Larry Schaltz's daughter. Her car
broke down some years back in the dead of winter in the middle
of nowhere. She walked across some fields to reach a
farmhouse that had a light on. Come to find out she had walked
clear across the frozen Missouri River and didn't even know it!
In the dim light, she thought it was just another frozen farm field.

In 2004, the Albrecht–Kemper Museum of Art will feature
local artist Thea Ide's "Local Landscapes of the Lewis and Clark
Trail." (816) 233-7003. www.albrecht-kemper.org. The Trails
West Festival will be in July of 2004. Admission is free. (800)
216-7080. www.StJoeArts.org. Learn about the region's Native
American heritage at the Sacred Hills Encampment in July at
the St. Joseph Riverfront: (816) 232-1240.

(800) 785-0360 • www.stjomo.com

Today's Trail

Explore the Sunset Grill & Rivertowne Resort
St. Joseph, Missouri

The Corps of Discovery camped in this vicinity on Saturday, July 7, 1804. On their way back, on September 6, 1806, the expedition met a trader from St. Louis near here and obtained a gallon of whiskey, allowing each member a little over three ounces—the first "spiritious licquor" they had drank since July 4, 1805.

Today, Sunset Grill Restaurant & Rivertowne Resort boasts an unequaled river view, excellent dining, unique lodging and a nice boat dock and fueling station. Located just minutes from town, this is an excellent "home base" while you check out the area highlights. Stay at one of the unique, modern-yet-rustic riverside cabins. Walk ten steps and dine at the Sunset Grill, where you can learn about the area's heyday of riverboat racing and water skiing. An interpretive Lewis & Clark sign is located here. 4012 River Road. For directions, dining and lodging information, call (816) 364-6500.

Rivertowne Resort is a collection of unique and modern-yet-rustic riverside cabins reminiscent of comfortable Colorado ski lodges.

Shown above are several points, trade beads and an original peace medal unearthed by Mike George of Oregon, Missouri. His lifetime passion for history has culminated in an incredible collection of more than 7,500 early Native American artifacts he has found primarily on the ground he farms around Oregon, Missouri. You may see him while you are traveling the trail. At Lewis & Clark events between Kansas City and St. Joseph, he oftentimes has a booth, and displays hundreds of rare points, beads and even an early peace medal that arrived on the scene shortly after Lewis & Clark went upriver. For information on his programs and his event schedule, call (660) 446-2216 or write P.O. Box 347, Oregon, Missouri, 64473.

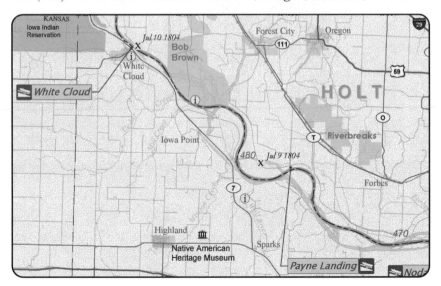

Nature's Curves Set in Steel

Not too far from the St. Joe riverfront is John Wiggington's Arrowhead Studios—Custom Designs of Iron & Steel. This local metalsmith has a gallery that will drop your jaw. John's inspiration from nature can be found throughout his studio. Check out his towering great blue heron and also his golden eagle with its 11-foot wingspan (covered with more than 1,700 metal feathers)—both made out of steel with the care of a surgeon. Another of my favorite creations in his gallery is his retired fire extinguisher turned into a bell. Its otherworldly Tibetan tones seem to both soothe the nerves and excite the imagination—conjuring thoughts of faraway lands. 611 Hickory Street. (816) 279-7359.

July 8, 1804

Today's Trail

Explore Monkey Mountain Park & Nature Reserve

Enjoy hiking two- and three-mile moderate trails here. You will traverse meadows, woods and limestone outcroppings with a beautiful view north at the summit. Call (816) 795-8200.

Expedition Entry

Near Monkey Mountain Park & Nature Reserve
Sunday, July 8, 1804

Today, Clark writes that Frazer is feeling much better. Five men are sick today with violent headaches and several with boils. The boats travel through a narrow channel about 45 to 80 yards wide, then pass the mouth of the "Nadawa River." Clark writes, "this Island Nadawa is the largest I have seen, formed by a Channel washing into the Nadawa River. 7-8,000 acres." The crew camps at the head of the island, after making a little over 12 miles today.

Expedition Entry

Monday, July 9, 1804

The crew makes 14 miles upriver today. Most notably, they pass an island on the starboard side, and then on the larboard side, Wolf River, about 60 yards wide, "navagable for Perogues Some destance up." The Corps sets up camp on the larboard side opposite the head of the island. Another party is camped on the opposite shore. When the other camp does not answer the crew's signals, the Corps suspects that the other camp might be a Sioux war party. The Corps fires the bow piece to alarm Corps members out hunting and "alled prepared to oppose if attacted."

Expedition Entry
Near White Cloud, Kansas
Tuesday, July 10, 1804

It turns out that the other camp was comprised of the expedition's hunters, who had turned in early and had not heard the opposite camp's attempts to signal them due to the hard blowing wind... "a mistake altogether," Clark writes. The crew eats on Solomon's Island, then proceeds on. "Opposite this island is a butifull bottom Prarie whuch will Contain about 2,000 acres of Land covered with wild rye & wild Potatoes." Clark notes a great number of goslings on the banks and ponds near the river and Captain Lewis kills two today. "Our men all getting well but much fatigued." The crew makes ten miles of progress today.

Today's Trail
Explore White Cloud, Kansas

White Cloud is home to an annual antique show like nothing you've ever seen before. Stop in at the local bank to admire the elegant steel scrollwork from the bank's earlier days.

While in town, be sure to say hello to Wolf River Bob, who almost single-handedly keeps White Cloud's history of Lewis & Clark alive. A riverfront shelter and Lewis & Clark marker are here, as well. If you get to visit with Wolf River Bob, ask about his early days working in Hollywood as an expert whip handler in western movies. While you are in the area, visit the George Ogden Community Center. On display is a remarkable bear claw necklace that predates Lewis & Clark by many generations.

Did you know that Earl Eastman holds a Kansas state record for catching a 90-pound flathead on the Missouri River? He uses goldfish for bait. Now in his 70s, Earl has been fishing the Missouri for at least 50 years.

July 11, 1804

Today's Trail
Explore Squaw Creek National Wildlife Refuge
Mound City, Missouri

Squaw Creek National Wildlife Refuge, a large 7,000-plus acre refuge, is a popular wintering area for bald eagles and snow geese. The refuge also includes some of the last remnants of native prairie. Throughout the year, the refuge provides resting, nesting and feeding habitat for more than 300 bird species. It also offers a glimpse of what much of the Missouri River floodplain once looked like. This is an excellent place for beginning birders. Events throughout the season increase your odds of sighting various birds with the assistance of the refuge staff. Hiking and driving tours are also available.

Camp or rent a lakeshore cabin at nearby Big Lake State Park, site of the expedition's camp on their return downriver on September 10, 1806 (see page 225). Boating, fishing and abundant waterfowl make this one of northwest Missouri's most popular parks. The park is located on Missouri's largest oxbow lake, formed when the Missouri River was channelized. A large marsh preserves an early Missouri landscape. Call (877) ICampMO.

(660) 442-3187 • http://midwest.fws.gov/SquawCreek

Expedition Entry
Wednesday, July 11, 1804

The crew sets out early again, passing a willow island and Little Tarkio Creek. Clark explores by land, finding shallow wetlands, dense undergrowth and vines so thick he can't get through. After walking three or four miles, Clark follows fresh horse tracks and locates a horse, standing alone on a sand beach. Clark assumes it had been left by some party of Oto hunting in the area. Seven deer are killed today (six by Drouillard alone). The expedition camps on an island opposite the Nemaha River after traveling six miles. Lewis takes astronomical observations tonight with his sextant.

Sandy banks, such as this one near Amazonia, Missouri, are generally only visible during low river levels. Peak flows tend to occur during spring's heavy rains and on into June. Winter flows are generally the lowest.

July 12, 1804

Today's Trail

Explore the Native American Heritage Museum
Highland, Kansas

Share in the journey of the Great Lakes Indians who were forced to emigrate to Kansas in the 1800s, adapting their traditional woodlands cultures to the rolling prairie landscape. At the museum, once a Presbyterian Mission built in 1845 to educate Iowa and Sac and Fox children, you will find quillwork, baskets and other artwork of present-day descendants of emigrant tribes. Through the interactive exhibits, Native Americans tell stories in their own words.

(785) 442-3304 • www.kshs.org/places/nativeamerican

Expedition Entry

Thursday, July 12, 1804

The Captains allow the men to rest today, while they take observations. After breakfast, Clark takes five men to explore up the Nemaha for about three miles. Clark goes ashore, through some prairie and climbs atop a knoll where he has "one of the most pleasing prospects I ever beheld…an emence, extensive & pleaseing prospect, of the Countrey around, I could See the meandering of the Little [Nemaha] River for at least 10 miles winding thro a meadow of 15 or 20,000 acres of high bottomland covered with Grass about 4½ feet high… the high lands were toped with Mounds or [ancient] Graves which is to me a Strong evidence of this Countrey haveing been thickly settled."

Clark notes that the Nemaha River is about 80 yards wide and that it heads up near the Pawnee village on River Blue, a branch of the Kansas. He writes, "thickets of Plumbs, Cheres, &c are Seen on its banks… observed great quantities of

Grapes, plums, Crab apples and a wild Cherry..." On the side of a sandstone cliff, Clark marks his name and day of the month. Alexander Willard is tried for sleeping on his post, for which he receives 25 lashes at sunset for the next four days. Hunters kill more deer today. Elk and buffalo are spotted.

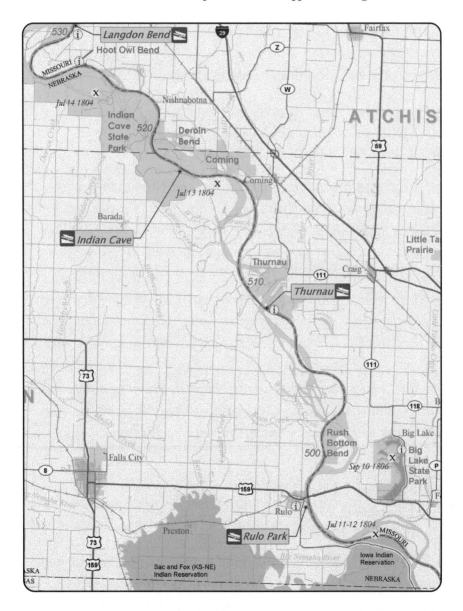

July 13, 1804

Expedition Entry
Friday, July 13, 1804

After being rocked by a violent storm during the night, the crew sets out at sunrise under a gentle breeze. After traveling two miles past Tarkio Creek, they pass St. Josephs Island. Clark notes a beautiful and extensive prairie covered with grass and abounding with grapes of "defferent kinds." The expedition logs 20 miles of progress today.

Expedition Entry
Saturday, July 14, 1804

Hard showers delay the crew's departure until 7 a.m. After setting out and traveling for an hour, "the atmispeir became Suddenly darkened by a blak & dismal looking Cloud... a Violent Storm... Struck the boat nearly broadside. The exerssions of all our Men who were out in an instant, aded to a Strong Cable and Anchor was Scrcely Sufficient to Keep the boat from being thrown up on the Sand Island, and dashed to pieces... in this Situation we continued for about 40 minits... this Storm Suddenly Seased & 1 minit the river was as Smoth as glass." Afterwards, the crew pushes on, passing the Nishnabotna River. Clark notes more grapes, plums and gooseberries. The Corps travels nine miles today.

Expedition Entry
Near Langdon, Missouri
Sunday, July 15, 1804

Today Clark travels overland across streams, across high prairies and past the Little Nemaha River. He swims across it, hikes another three miles, and then waits for the boats to arrive. *Clark sees great quantities of grapes, plums, wild cherries, hazelnuts and gooseberries. They travel almost ten miles.*

Expedition Entry
Near Star School Hill Prairie, Missouri
Monday, July 16, 1804

After setting out early, the crew passes several small islands. The boat runs atop a sawyer. After making 20 miles today, they camp in some woods on the larboard side on an island. The river is falling, Clark notes.

Expedition Entry
Tuesday, July 17, 1804

The crew rests today, so that the Captains can ascertain the longitude and get the chronometer corrected. Several men are sent out to hunt. Captain Lewis returns from a hike, noting "hand Som Countrey, the Creek near the high land is rapid and nearly as muddy as the river, & rising." One crewmember catches "two verry fat Cat fish." Four deer are killed today. The men camp in the "Bald Pated Prarie," and the next day, they leave the land that will become Missouri.

The Captain Lewis *is a retired dredge boat that now houses the Museum of Missouri River History. Check it out in Brownville, Nebraska.*

Today's Trail
Explore Brownville, Nebraska

If you are a fan of picture-perfect river hamlets, you will be intrigued by this small town's charm. Bookstores, antique shops, a winery and a riverboat ride await. Tour the *Captain Meriwether Lewis,* a retired dredge boat that now houses the Museum of Missouri River History. Take a river excursion aboard the Spirit of Brownville: (402) 825-6441. And ask about the yearly River Rat Reunion in August. Be sure to visit the Palmerton Art Gallery and the park, too: www.brownville-ne.com.

Another must-visit in the area is Indian Cave State Park in nearby Shubert, Nebraska. I love this place. You can spend a whole day or even a weekend exploring this extensive park. The forested rolling hills offer extensive campgrounds, nice river views, many trails, and a walkway along a large sandstone cave, covered with the names of river travelers dating back to the mid-1800s. Petroglyphs etched on the walls of the cave are the only known examples of their kind found in Nebraska. Their cultural origin and age remain a mystery. The petroglyphs depict

forms, shapes and scenes, most of the elements of nature and mostly wildlife. The cave is easily accessible to park visitors. This is one site you won't want to miss.

(402) 883-2575
www.ngpc.state.ne.us/parks/
icave.html

Jane Smith is the only woman riverboat pilot operating on the Missouri River today. She pilots the Spirit of Brownville *Excursion Boat.*

Today's Trail

Explore Rock Port, Missouri

Stop in at the Star Hill Prairie Art Center at 210 Main Street and talk to Clarence Schaffner to find out the goings-ons in Rock Port. There are a number of retired men in town who, in their younger days, channelized the Missouri River for the Corps of Engineers. Strike up a conversation at the local diner and you may hear some great river stories: (660) 744-5800.

Below, Dick Bowen, a resident of Rock Port, displays photographs from his career spent channelizing the Missouri River, from 1939 to 1973. His starting wage was 50 cents an hour. He saw the original river as it was before the channelization efforts began here. "When it was a mile wide and a foot deep."

He's built tugboats, run pile drivers, wheeled rock and helped make huge mile-long mats out of willow to reduce bank erosion. "We felt we could do it, it had to be done, and we did it," Bowen said. "It was a lot of long, hard hours, but those jobs were the salvation for a lot of families." When I asked him about the muddiness, he said, "there's no comparison. It was so much muddier back then—a regular pail of water dipped into the river would have 4 inches of mud in it."

After leaving present-day Missouri, the expedition successfully reached the Pacific Ocean and explored countless miles out West. The expedition crossed the state of Missouri once more on their way back downriver to St. Louis. Their journal entries from the return expedition are highlighted on the next pages.

Region Review

Return Downriver to St. Louis
Ready to Be Home At Last

September 9 – 23, 1806

Eager to get back to St. Louis and home, the crew travels quickly over their last 600 miles on the Missouri River—more than 70 miles on some days—the crew "plying thear ores with great dexterity," Clark writes.

They were so anxious to return, that they often skipped hunting, preferring to scour the banks for pawpaws. Drams of whiskey, spiritous singing late into the night, almost daily encounters with other boatmen and, finally, reaching those westernmost settlements as they neared St. Louis were daily reminders that their epic adventure was drawing to a close. As they drew ever closer to St. Louis, even sightings of the mundane, such as a cow in a pasture, were sure to raise hollers from the crew—eager for any sign of a settlement.

Traveling downriver in their slim dugout canoes, dressed in buckskins, the travel-weary group must have been quite a sight for the onlookers cheering their arrival in St. Charles on Sunday, September 21.

Note to readers: Since the upriver portion of this guidebook included highlights of select communities, in this next section, I have omitted the "Today's Trail" references so that I can devote this space to more of Clark's journal entries uninterrupted. Please refer to the previous pages for modern-day trail stops, historic sites and communities that you won't want to miss while traveling the Lewis & Clark Trail in Missouri.

Northwest corner of the state of Missouri
Tuesday, September 9, 1806

Today, after setting out early at 8 a.m., now on their return journey downriver, the expedition passes the present Iowa-Missouri state line. The Corps passes the entrance of the Platte River. Clark notes the low turbulent water and writes, "below the River Platt the Current of the Missouri becomes evidently more rapid than above and the Snags much more noumerous and bad to pass."

Late in the evening, the crew camps at the "Bald pated prairie," which Clark had first noted on July 16, 1804, on their trip up the Missouri River. Clark notes that the "musquetors are yet troublesom, tho' not So much So as they were above the River platt. the Climate is every day preceptably wormer and air more Sultery than I have experienced for a long time." He observes, "our party appears extreamly anxious to get to their Country and friends." Clark goes on to write that Captain Lewis has recovered from being accidentally shot in the thigh by one of the hunters in August. "His wounds are heeled up and he Can walk and even run nearly as well as ever he Could." The crew travels 73 miles downriver today before making camp.

At Big Lake State Park
Big Lake, Missouri
Wednesday, September 10, 1806

The Corps sets out under a moderate wind. The crew meets three Frenchmen heading upriver in a small pirogue, to trade with the Pania Luup (or Wolf Indians) located at the Platte River. Clark writes, "this man was extreemly friendly to us he offered us any thing he had, we axcepted of a bottle of whisky only which we gave to our party." Clark listens to the news of

September 11, 1806

Zebulon Pike's explorations on the Mississippi River, as well as his current trip up the Arkansas River.

Clark writes "proceeded on through a very bad part of the river Crouded with Snags & Sawyers and incamped on a Sand bar about 4 miles above the Grand Nemahar. we find the river in this timbered Country narrow and more moveing Sands and a much greater quantity of Sawyers or Snags than above. Great caution and much attention is required to Stear Clear of all those dificuelties in this low State of the water. we Saw Deer rackoons and turkies on the Shores to day one of the men killed a racoon which the indians very much admired." The crew travels 65 miles downriver today.

Near Amazonia, Missouri
Thursday, September 11, 1806

The Corps travels 40 miles downriver today. The crew stops before the Nodaway River to send out six hunters, since all of their meat has spoiled. The hunters are only able to bring in two deer, despite seeing a lot of deer sign. Clark notes "the mosquitoes are no longer troublesome on the river, from what cause they are noumerous above and not So on this part of the river I cannot account." Clark writes in some detail about the "wolves howling in different directions... the barking of the little prarie wolves resembled those of our Common Small Dogs that ¾ of our party believed them to be the dogs of Some boat assending which was yet below us... The papaws nearly ripe."

Opposite page: Leonard McAfee, who lives right next to the river in Amazonia, Missouri, is one of the few remaining commercial fishermen on the Missouri River.

St. Joseph, Missouri
Friday, September 12, 1806

After proceeding on at dawn and making seven miles of headway, the crew encounters more trappers paddling up the Missouri River. One pirogue from St. Louis is heading up to trade with the "Panias on River Platt," and the other boat is bound further upriver to trade with the Mahars.

At St. Michael's Prairie (present-day St. Joseph, Missouri), Clark reunites with two French interpreters who had assisted the expedition previously. They include Pierre Dorian, a Sioux interpreter, and Joseph Gravelines. Gravelines served on the expedition during the winter at Fort Mandan. In the spring of 1805, Gravelines escorted an Arikara Chief to Washington, D.C., to meet President Jefferson at the bequest of the Captains. Clark wrote "Gravelin was ordered to the Ricaras with a Speech from the president of the U. States to that nation and some present which had been given the Ricara Chief who had visited the U. States and unfortunately died at the City of Washington."

Clark also advised Gravelines to extend his invitation to a dozen chiefs, including the Yanktons, to return with him to visit Washington the following spring. Clark writes, "the evening proveing to be wet and Cloudy we Concluded to continue all night, we despatched the two Canoes a head to hunt with 5 hunters in them."

Saturday, September 13, 1806

Each man is given a dram of whiskey and they set out after sunrise. By 8 a.m., they reunite with the five hunters, who have not caught any game. A hard wind from the southeast prevents them from proceeding "through the emecity of Snags which was imediately below." In a few hours, the hunters bring in four deer and a turkey, despite complaints of rushes so high and thick that it is virtually impossible to hunt. They make 18 miles today, "the day disagreeably worm."

Sunday, September 14, 1806

The crew sets out early and stays on the ready for a likely encounter with the Kansa, or Kaw Indians. The Kansa guard this stretch of river and board any vessel heading upriver to trade with other tribes. They often exact a bribe for passage or rob the boats outright. All deckhands are prepared for the possibility of seeing action today. Should the Kansa try to board the boat, Clark writes "we are deturmined not to allow... for the smallest insult we Shall fire on them." At 2 p.m., below the old Kansa village, the Corps meets three large boats bound for trade with the Yanktons and Mahars. Clark writes "those young men received us with great friendship and pressed on us Some whisky for our men, Bisquet, Pork and Onions & part of their Stores, we continued near 2 hours with those boats, making every enquirey into the state of our friends and country."

As they pass further downriver, they count 37 deer on the banks. After descending 53 miles, they stop on an island below their encampment of July 1, 1804. Clark writes "our party received a dram and Sung Songs untill 11 oClock at night in the greatest harmoney."

Near Missouri City, Missouri
Monday, September 15, 1806

After setting out early under a stiff headwind, they see several deer swimming in the river. At 11 a.m. they pass the mouth of the Kansas River and note the future site of Kansas City's Case Park and Lewis & Clark monument. "About a mile below we landed and Capt Lewis and my Self assended a hill which appeared to have a Commanding Situation for a fort, the Shore is bold and rocky immediately at the foot of the hill, from the top of the hill you have a perfect Command of the river, this hill fronts the Kanzas and has a view of the Missouri a Short distance above that river. we landed one time only to let the men geather Pappaws or the Custard apple of which this Country abounds, and the men are very fond of." *Several hunters team up to hunt and kill a small elk on an island, which they promptly butchered. Due to strong winds throughout the day, they descend only 49 miles. Clark notes* "we passd Some of the most Charming bottom lands to day... the weather disagreeably worm... we Should be almost Suficated Comeing out of a northern Country open and Cool... in which we had been for nearly two years, rapidly decending into a woody Country in a wormer Climate... is probably the Cause of our experiencing the heat much more... than those who have Continued within [it]..."

Tuesday, September 16, 1806

After setting out early and proceeding "tolerably well," *the day proves to be* "excessively worm and disagreeable." *The men row very little, apathetic due to the heat. At 10 a.m. they meet a large trading pirogue bound for the Panias Tribe. Then at 11 a.m. they meet young Joseph Robidoux, with a* "boat of six ores and 2 Canoes," *bound for trade with the Panias,*

Mahars and Otoes. Robidoux, whose family had been leaders in the fur trade for several generations, had established a trading post at the site of St. Joseph in 1800 and is thus regarded as St. Joe's founder. The Corps then proceeds on to an island above their encampment from the 16ʰ and 17ʰ of June 1804, having traveled 52 miles today.

Near Miami, Missouri
Wednesday, September 17, 1806

After setting out as usual, the Corps passes the island of the little Osage village, considered by Clark's navigator to be the worst place on the river. Clark writes, "at this place water of the Missouri is confined between an Island and the SE main Shore and passes through a narrow chanel for more than 2 miles which is crouded with Snags in maney places quite across obligeing the navigater to pick his passage between those Snags as he can, in maney places the current passing with great velocity against the banks which cause them to fall."

At 11 a.m. the party meets Captain McClellan and his crew in a large boat, heading upriver. Clark notes that McClellan, "was Somewhat astonished to See us return and appeared rejoiced to meet us... this Gentleman informed us that we had been long Since given out by the people of the U S Generaly and almost forgotten, the President of the U. States had yet hopes of us..." In his own journal, Sergeant Ordway wrote that McClellan had told them "the people in general in the United States were concerned about us as they had heard that we were all killed, then again they heard that the Spanyards had us in the mines..." The Corps descends 30 miles today, camping four miles above the Grand River on the southeast side.

Thursday, September 18, 1806

The crew rises early, passing the Grand River at 7 a.m. At 10 a.m. they stop to gather paw paws to eat. "We have nothing but a fiew Buisquit to eate and are partly compelled to eate poppows which we find in great quanitites on the Shores, the weather we found excessively hot as usial. The lands fine particularly the bottoms," Clark writes. They find the current here much more gentle than it was two years prior, when they were traveling upriver. They see little game today: one deer, a bear at a distance and three turkeys. "Our party entirely out of provisions Subsisting on poppaws. we divide the buiskits which amounted to nearly one buiskit per man, this in addition to the poppaws is to last down to the Settlement's which is [at least] 150 miles. The party appear perfectly contented and tell us that they can live very well on the pappaws." Crew members complain of sore eyes. The Corps travels 52 miles today.

At Clark's Hill/Norton State Historic Site
Near Jefferson City, Missouri
Friday, September 19, 1806

Today, the men ply their oars and "we decended with great velocity," stopping only once briefly to gather pawpaws. "Our anxiety as also the wish of the party to proceed on as expeditiously as possible… enduce us to continue on without halting to hunt." Clark calculates that the first settlement they will encounter is still 140 miles downriver. They hope to reach it in two days. The crew manages to cover 72 miles today, setting up for the night at the confluence with the Osage River, where they had camped on June 1 and 2, 1804. Clark writes, "a very singular disorder is takeing place amongst our party that of the Sore eyes. three of the party have their eyes inflamed and Sweled in Such a manner as to render them extreamly painfull, particularly when exposed to the light, the eye ball is much inflaimed and the lid appears burnt with the Sun... from it's Sudden appearance I am willing to believe it may be owing to the reflection of the Sun on the water."

Near Marthasville, Missouri
Saturday, September 20, 1806

This morning, three crewmen are unable to row due to the sorry state of their eyes. "We found it necessary to leave one of our Crafts and divide the men into the other Canoes," *Clark writes. They pass the mouth of the Osage and then the Gasconade River. They also pass five Frenchmen on a pirogue heading upriver.* "The party being extreemly anxious to get down ply their ores very well, we Saw Some cows on the bank which was a joyfull Sight to the party and Caused a Shout to be raised for joy."

Later in the day, they came upon a little French village called La Charette. "The men raised a Shout and Sprung upon their ores and we soon landed opposite to the village. our party requested to be permitted to fire off their Guns which was alowed & they discharged three rounds with a harty cheer, which was returned from five tradeing boats which lay opposite the village..." *The Captains quickly procure pork, beef and whiskey for the crew.*

Clark writes, "every person, both French and americans Seem to express great pleasure at our return, and acknowledged them selves much astonished in Seeing us return. they informed us that we were Supposed to have been lost long Since..."

The crew travels 68 miles downriver today.

St. Charles, Missouri
Sunday, September 21, 1806

The Corps sets out at 7:30 a.m. They pass 12 canoes of Kickapoos ascending the river on a hunting expedition. Clark writes, "Saw Several persons also Stock of different kind on the bank which reviv'd the party very much. At 4 p.m. we arived in Sight of St. Charles, the party rejoiced at the Sight of this hospitable village plyed thear ores with great dexterity and we Soon arived opposite the Town, this day being Sunday we observed a number of Gentlemen and ladies walking on the bank, we Saluted the Village by three rounds from our blunderbuts and the Small arms of the party, and landed near the lower part of the town. we were met by great numbers of the inhabitants, we found them excessively polite... the inhabitants of this village appear much delighted at our return and seem to vie with each other in their politeness to us all." The Corps travels 48 miles downriver today.

St. Louis, Missouri
Monday, September 22, 1806

Clark writes, "this morning being very wet and the rain Still Continueing hard, and our party being all Sheltered in the houses of those hospitable people, we did not think proper to proceed on untill after the rain was over." Clark takes this opportunity to write to his friends in Kentucky. Then at 10 a.m., the rain ceased and "we Collected our party and Set out and proceeded on down to the Contonement [Fort Bellefontaine], at Coldwater Creek about 3 miles up the Missouri on it's Southern banks... we were kindly received by the Gentlemen of this place... we were honored with a Salute of Guns and a harty welcom."

Jefferson National Expansion Memorial
St. Louis, Missouri
Tuesday, September 23, 1806

The crew rises early, sets out and descends the Missouri River to the Mississippi River and down it to the St. Louis riverfront, where they arrive at about 12 o'clock. Clark writes, "we were met by all the village and received a harty welcom from it's inhabitants... we accepted of the invitation of Mr. Peter Chouteau and partook a room in his house... we payed a friendly visit to... Some of our old friends this evening..." In his journal, Ordway adds "the people gathred on the Shore and Huzzared three cheers."

September 1806:

Home At Last

And so the epic expedition of two years and four months drew to a close. They had traveled close to 8,000 miles and lost only one man, apparently due to appendicitis. During that time, they literally filled in the map of the western frontier and paved the way for the building of a nation in the newly acquired Louisiana Territory.

From their beginning at Wood River, Illinois, in 1804, to their trials and tribulations all the way to the Pacific Ocean and their return to St. Louis, Missouri, in 1806, the hearty members of the Corps of Discovery had faced every hardship and deprivation known to man and had endured.

The Expedition's
Legacy in Missouri

Late on a quiet Sunday afternoon, weary crew members, dressed entirely in buckskin, fired a three-gun salute as they eddied out of the main current of the Mighty Missouri and nosed their dugout canoes into the muddy banks of St. Charles, Missouri. Two days later, on September 23, 1806, they arrived to great fanfare at St. Louis, their final destination. The whole town turned out to welcome the returning explorers. "The party is considerably rejoiced that we have the expedition completed," Captain Lewis wrote.

In part forgotten, even given up for dead, the Corps of Discovery's return cannot be summed up easily. Although in modern times we have come to accept the legendary status of the expedition, 200 years ago things were not so cut and dried. Though the sheer fact they survived should have been reason enough for celebration, for the Captains, the return was surely met with mixed feelings. For one, the expedition had failed to find a navigable waterway to the Pacific.

But due to the duration of the trip, and the fact that only one man died, one historian has called the odyssey "the most successful military expedition in U.S. history." And perhaps just as important to our fledgling nation as actually finding a waterway, Lewis & Clark have become icons for the seemingly unquenchable American desire to explore and to head West. They have become heroes—something every country needs.

Having written a total of more than 1.5 million words in their journals, they were able to record an important moment in time for our country. They had met countless Native American tribes, recording their way of life in an era while they were still relatively untouched by what was to come.

We know all of this now, but at the moment of their return, the wilderness-hardened explorers must have experienced mild culture shock with the sudden fame, and the return to the easy accommodations of civilization. Just as their lives were now written into the legacy of the West, soon they would branch out and leave their impression on every aspect of life in the United States, becoming everything from farmers to politicians. Their time in the wilderness had helped to mold the character and confidence of the men, which is reflected in the extraordinary adventures that many of the men would continue to seek out for the rest of their lives.

The men were paid and discharged on October 10, 1806. Some crewmembers returned to their families and farms, while others turned to the frontier's allures again, this time heading for the wealth and adventures to be found in the burgeoning beaver trade. But the roots of many of the men grew deeper during their time along the Missouri River and many chose to make what would become the state of Missouri their home.

A Return to Family, Friends, Politics & More...

What follows is a recounting of where the crewmembers went and what they did after the expedition. Records are very spotty, as you will soon see.

Meriwether Lewis was committed to the shared leadership with William Clark until the very end, even when Washington officials were preparing bonus rewards for members of the expedition. Since Lewis was technically a higher ranking officer than Clark, he was rewarded 1,600 acres whereas Clark was given only 1,000. True to his convictions, Lewis rebelled against this unfair decision until Washington rethought, rewarding Clark the same amount of land as Lewis, 1,600 acres.

Soon after their return, Captain Lewis was appointed by the President to become Governor of the Louisiana territory. Far from the "simpler" days on the expedition, his duties now included unraveling unsolvable political problems, including disputed French, Spanish and American land titles. The bitter antagonism of the jealous Secretary of the Territory only magnified the situation. After two years as Governor, several of Lewis' drafts as Governor, as well as some he made during the expedition, were put under question by Washington clerks. In order to set things straight, settle expenses and get the ball rolling on the publication of expedition journals, Lewis made his way to Washington in the fall of 1809. Unfortunately, for a man already known for moods of melancholy, the problems and accusations he intended to take care of caused him great emotional strain. On October 11, 1809, while on the Natchez Trace, Lewis died from either murder or suicide. A monument in his honor stands at his burial place near Hohenwald, Tennessee.

Early in 1807, 2nd Lieutenant William Clark was made primary Indian Agent for the Louisiana territory and based his work out of St. Louis, on the grounds where the St. Louis Arch is now located. Many Native Americans would travel to St. Louis to see him to share the grievances they had in varying disputes with the white man. He was also appointed to Brigadier General of the Louisiana Militia, and remained in this and the Indian Agent position until his death. Clark married his childhood sweetheart, Julia Hancock from Fincastle, Virginia, and the two happy newlyweds took their honeymoon on the Ohio River on January 5, 1808. Julia and William Clark had four sons, the first of whom they named Meriwether Lewis Clark and one daughter. Unfortunately, 12 years later, on June 27, 1820, Julia died of illness at her parent's residence.

While his wife was still alive, in June 1813, Clark was appointed Governor of the Louisiana territory after his friend and partner Meriwether Lewis died on the Natchez Trace. Clark served as Territorial Governor until 1820. He failed to win the first election for governor in 1820 after Missouri gained statehood. Clark remarried Harriet Kennerly, the widow of Dr. John Radford and the cousin of Clark's first wife, Julia. With his second wife, Clark had two sons, but only one lived past childhood. On September 1, 1838, at the age of 68 years old, Clark died, leaving people in the belief that he was the oldest American settler in St. Louis. Clark was buried with full military honors in Bellefontaine Cemetery in St. Louis, Missouri.

After the return of the expedition, Clark had "Pompey," Sacagawea's young son, whose true name was Jean Baptiste, and Sacagawea's daughter, Lizette, brought to his home in St. Louis where Clark could be his guardian and raise him. In November 2000, over 150 years after his death, Clark was finally appointed co-captain of the expedition.

York, Clark's slave, was finally freed by Clark in 1811, and he then married in Kentucky. Always worried about York's well-being,

Clark gave him six horses and a dray, which he used to start a wagon freight company. The freight business transported between Nashville, Tennessee, and Richmond, Kentucky, but had failed by 1832. On his way to visit Clark, York died of cholera in Tennessee.

While on his way home, on August 13, 1806, Private John Colter was discharged from the Army with honors. With trappers Forest Handcock and Joseph Dickson, Colter went back to Yellowstone, remaining with them for around six months. After half of a year together, there was a falling out between the three. Colter arrived at the Platte River mouth by July. He entered the Manuel Lisa trapping party and with them started back for Yellowstone. Colter was there by October of 1807, trapped for several years.

While out west, Colter had headed up the Missouri River into Blackfeet Indian territory. Because Colter had been friends with the Crows, the enemy of the Blackfeet, he had been in many fights with the tribe. During his years of trapping in the area, he is said to have scalped nearly 101 Blackfeet Indians. After meeting up with John Potts at the Three Forks, the two encountered 800 Blackfeet Indians. Potts, who did not want to be taken prisoner, was killed by Blackfeet arrows. Afterward, Colter was taken prisoner by the Indians, who stripped him of his clothes and, after he claimed he was a bad runner, told him to run for his life. The Blackfeet then pursued him like he was a hunted animal, giving him only a 400-yard head start. Colter, who was actually an adept hunter, ran with so much speed that he quickly separated himself from the angry Blackfeet.

As some of the pack gained on him, Colter ran harder, dripping blood from his nose and mouth, from cuts as well as from effort. With only a mile between himself and the river, Colter faced a spear bearing Indian. He wrestled the Indian to the ground, then dispatched him with his own weapon. Colter found a place to hide in a mound of driftwood in the river. He traveled constantly with hardly any sleep or rest, stopping mostly for meals consisting of tree bark and roots. Eleven days after the attack, Colter arrived at the fort with misshapen, swollen feet.

In his flight, Colter became the first man to witness Yellowstone's geyser eruptions, a phenomenon many people believed to be a lie. After his story, Yellowstone Park became known as Colter's Hell for some time.

Colter then returned to St. Louis by May of 1809. While in St. Louis, he sold his land warrant to John G. Comegys, a land investor.

In 1810, Colter married an Indian woman known as Sallie and the two moved to a farm close to Charette, Franklin County, Missouri. Colter and Sallie had one son whom they named Hiram.

Colter designed a map of the Northwest, which he gave to William Clark. He also tried to collect $377.60 from Meriwether Lewis' estate on May 28, 1811, probably for extra pay from the Corps of Discovery, but since the estate was bankrupt, his attempt was unsuccessful. Colter died on November 22, 1813, and was buried near his home, at Dundee, Missouri, on Tunnel Hill.

In December 1814, after Colter's death, his possessions went up for auction, but raised only $124.44½. This money went to Sallie. His widowed wife also received $69 more on January 9, 1815. She remarried sometime and died after 1822.

On September 29, 1806, Sergeant John Ordway witnessed the sales of John Collins and Joseph Whitehouse's land warrants. He also bought the warrants of William Werner and Jean Baptiste La Page, fellow members of the expedition. Afterwards, Ordway accompanied Lewis and a party of Indians to visit the President in Washington. Ordway made his own way to New Hampshire, and then settled in the Tywappity Bottom near New Madrid, Missouri, in 1809. Ordway gained land, including two plantations with peach and apple orchards, which both earned a fair amount of profit. In the meantime, Ordway married a woman named Gracy, but he then died in 1817 with no children.

After the return of the expedition, interpreter George Drouillard settled in Cape Girardeau. He also bought the land warrants of John Collins and Joseph Whitehouse. With the sale of these warrants and other properties under his name, Drouillard earned $1,300 on April 3, 1807. Drouillard soon made a trip back to the Rocky Mountains, taking fantastic topographical notes on the mountain country, which he gave to William Clark. Clark took these details and used them in his map of the Northwest. In 1810, while with the Manuel Lisa Party, Drouillard was killed by the Blackfeet Indians at the Three Forks, where he had helped construct a trading post. Coincidentally, Drouillard had encountered the violence of the Blackfeet Indians some time before while on an expedition to the Upper Marias River.

In 1809, Meriwether Lewis loaned money to Private Hugh Hall, who was reported to be in St. Louis, Missouri. Hall was said to still be living in 1828.

In May 1808, Private Thomas Proctor Howard departed Fort Adams with Captain Stark's Infantry. Howard married Genevieve

Roy in St. Louis, Missouri, and the two had a son named Joseph.

After the expedition, Private Hugh McNeal stayed in the Army until 1811. Clark listed him as dead by 1825 – 1828.

On July 5, 1832, Private John Newman married Olympia Dubreuil of St. Louis, Missouri, daughter of Elisabeth and Antoine Dubreuil. From 1834 to 1838, Newman traded on the upper part of the Missouri River. He was killed in the spring season of 1838 by the Yankton Sioux Indians.

In 1807, Meriwether Lewis wrote that he considered Private Moses Reed to be an excellent addition to the expedition. At this time, Reed received $180 in back pay and $178.50 in bonus pay. Like the other expedition members, Reed was given a land warrant, which was for property in Franklin County, Missouri. After the expedition, he trapped for a year with his relative Daniel Boone, then with Squire Boone in Indiana. Reed died in December 1809 and was survived by his wife, Nancy, and daughter, Janette. Reed is most likely buried in Little Flock Baptist Burying Grounds in Harrison County, Indiana.

On March 11, 1807, Meriwether Lewis sent Private William Werner $30.75, a horse, saddle and other items valued at $44.50. Under the conditions of this arrangement, William Clark was instructed to deduct the price of the horse from Werner's pay if the animal died of negligence, but not if it happened to die from any other cause. The money was also supposed to be taken from Werner's pay if he sold the horse to someone else. For some time after the expedition's return, Werner assisted Clark as an Indian agent in Missouri. By 1828, Werner was reported to be alive in Virginia.

Private Joseph Whitehouse sold his bonus land warrant of 160 acres to George Drouillard for $280. In 1807, he was arrested in St. Louis for debt, but was a free man by 1812, when he joined the Army to serve in the war. Five years later, Whitehouse deserted his station.

Private John Boley was part of Warfington's 1805 return party to St. Louis, Missouri. On August 9, 1805, he joined Zebulon Pike's party, which was searching for the sources of the Mississippi River. Boley also went with Pike to the Rocky Mountains, but arrived in New Orleans, Louisiana, in February 1807 with a party that went down the Arkansas River. After his parents died, Boley inherited their home and property located in Meramac, Missouri. Some people believe that Boley was part of the Bissell brothers' expedition to the mountains. It is known that Boley and his wife were living in Carondelet, Missouri, in October 1823.

Private Robert Frazier went to Washington and Virginia with Meriwether Lewis, but he returned to St. Louis, Missouri, and was given a land warrant on October 6, 1806. Frazier was in the militia serving against the Aaron Burr plotters in St. Louis and New Orleans. He had found evidence of treason and was a witness at the trial. Until 1815, Frazier had a few reported run-ins with the St. Louis law. From 1825, he lived near the Gasconade River in Missouri, and then died in Franklin County, Missouri in 1837. During his life, Frazier drew maps of the Northwest that he intended to publish with his journal of the expedition. These maps are now in the Library of Congress.

Private Joseph Barter may be the same man known as Joseph La Liberte who married Julie Village on January 11, 1835, in St. Louis, Missouri. La Liberte died at the age of 60 and was buried in St. Louis on May 31, 1837.

Private Francois (William) Labiche went with Meriwether Lewis to Washington, acting as an interpreter for the group of Indians they were accompanying. Labiche may be the same man known as Francois Labuche, who married a Genevieve Flore and baptized seven kids in St. Louis, Missouri, between 1811 and 1834. Labiche was reported to be alive in St. Louis after 1828.

Toussaint Charbonneau worked under Manuel Lisa and William Clark as an interpreter while Clark was the head of Indian Affairs. Charbonneau probably lived until the 1830s.

While escorting Chief Shahaka home, Private George Shannon lost one of his legs and received a pension for the loss. He practiced law in Kentucky and then became active in Missouri politics. Shannon died in 1836.

Private John Shields joined his relative Daniel Boone in a trapping trip in Missouri. Afterward, he settled in Indiana and then died in 1809.

Certainly, the Lewis and Clark expedition had been the greatest adventure many of these men would see in their lives. The crew of the Corps of Discovery wove seamlessly into many diverse aspects of that new material—that new West—that would forever change the American flag.

Camping at Missouri
Conservation Areas & State Parks

The following pages offer an overview of where primitive camping on conservation areas is allowed along the river. They are listed here in their entirety because, due to the bicentennial, many of these areas now allow river-approach camping through 2006. River-approach camping is generally very primitive (no water or restrooms). Campgrounds at state parks, which generally have fire rings, showers, toilets and shelters, are not listed on the following table. Access that information by calling the Department of Natural Resources at (800) 334-6946 or go online to www.mostateparks.com. You can also call (877) ICampMO to request information or to make a reservation at state park campgrounds throughout the state.

The following table is available online for download at www.moriver.org. I am including it here verbatim from the Missouri Department of Conservation. I have bolded the new river-approach camping information below, which is of special interest to Lewis & Clark Trail river explorers.

As the Lewis and Clark Bicentennial commemoration progresses along Missouri's rivers and highways, travelers will pass conservation areas and accesses. Most areas have frontage on the river, but some are a few miles back, perhaps on the Katy Trail or the highway trail designated by familiar brown and white signs. Rules vary from area to area for many good reasons, but this document is designed to clarify and summarize those most critical to Lewis and Clark Trail travelers. The following rules apply to smaller parties, but groups of ten or more wanting to camp, conduct events, moor overnight, etc. should contact the department for a special use permit. Conservation areas on the trail generally have one of five camping rules:
  • Closed to all camping
  • Contact another managing entity (e.g. ramps located in city parks) for camping information
  • Primitive camping in designated areas only
  • Dispersed primitive camping

• Primitive river-approach-camping. **River-approach camping is new, and is permitted only through 2006. It allows visitors traveling by boat, from April 1 to September 30, to camp on any clear site within 100 yards of the river, unless posted as closed to camping.** The April 1 to September 30 limitation reflects the heavy usage of most areas for hunting and trapping activities during the fall and winter seasons.

Conservation areas are not campgrounds with developed sites, so expect only "primitive camping" on these areas: space only, with no other amenities, and on a first-come-first-serve basis. Primitive camp users must adhere to all regulations and must remove all trash, properly dispose of human waste, contain fires and extinguish them on departure, and not cut standing trees, shrubs or brush. Overnight mooring adjacent to river-approach-camping camps and outside the navigation channel is allowed.

Touring groups using river-approach-camping sites may allow over-land support teams to camp with them (walk-in) but not bring vehicles off of the road or parking lots. Groups of more than ten should obtain a special use permit from the area manager.

Boat access: MDC owns or helped communities develop almost 50 boat ramps along the Lewis & Clark Trail in Missouri. They are first-come-first-serve facilities, with users expected to quickly clear the ramp area, park in designated areas and be patient.

These areas are closed to commercial activities, but we do allow fuel delivery trucks to deliver fuel at any access on request from a boater. Similarly, commercial services providing sanitary pumpout, water delivery, etc. may use the ramps to service the requests of boaters. Expeditions and tour boats may drop gang-planks at ramps to load or unload passengers, but must not moor for more than 15 minutes in any way that impedes access by other users.

The following table is organized in the order Lewis and Clark might have come across them. Areas that might once have been on the river may be separated today, and remember that the expedition was not just on water: at all times in Missouri, a land crew hunted for food, vantage points and information that could take them several miles away from the water. Additional information on the areas listed may be found in the *Conservation Atlas,* at www.mdc.state.mo.us/atlas/

When an entry cites "river mile," it is at the boat ramp (if there is one) or best site to access the area by boat. Areas on tributaries report the mile of the tributary mouth. Date citations reflect the date when the boats of the Lewis & Clark expedition passed near the area.

Area	River Mile	Expedition passed	Boat Connection	Interpretive Sign	Camping Rules
Bird's Blue Hole	0	11-19-03 :	none		no camping
Commerce Access	39	11-22-03 :	bank	yes*	contact City of Commerce
Headwaters Access	49	11-23-03 :	ramp		contact Little River Drainage District
Red Star Access	53	11-23-03 :	ramp	yes*	no camping
Juden Creek CA	inland	11-24-03 :	none		no camping
Apple Creek CA	Apple Cr.	11-25-03 :	ramp	yes	designated areas
Tower Rock CA	80	11-25-03 :	bank	yes	no camping
Seventy-six CA	91	11-26-03 :	bank		designated areas
Red Rock Landing	94	11-27-03 :	bank		designated areas
St. Mary's Access	inland	11-28-03 :	ramp		contact City of St. Mary's
Marina de Gabouri Access	122	12-03-03 :	ramp*	yes*	contact City of Ste. Genevieve
Magnolia Hollow CA	129	12-04-03 :	bank	yes	river-approach-camping; dispersed camping year around, designated during deer season
Truman Park Access	141	12-5-03 :	ramp		no camping
Teszars Woods/Flamm Access	Meramec	12-6-03 :	ramp*		no camping
North Riverfront Park Access	189	12-12-03 :	ramp		contact St. Louis City Parks
Columbia Bottom CA	3 (0-5)	5-14-04 9-23-06	ramp	yes (two)	river-approach-camping
Pelican Island Access	11	5-15-04 9-22-06	ramp		river-approach-camping
Pelican Island CA	11-16	5-15-04 9-22-06	bank		river-approach-camping
St. Stanislaus CA	22	5-16-04 9-22-06	bank	yes	river-approach-camping
Blanchette Landing Access	27	5-16-04 9-22-06	ramp		Contact City of St. Charles
Riverwoods CA	29	5-20-04 9-21-06	bank		river-approach-camping
Howell Island CA	45-49	5-22-04 9-21-06	bank		river-approach-camping
Weldon Spring CA	48	5-23-04 9-21-06	ramp	yes	river-approach-camping
Engelman Woods NA	inland (55)	5-24-04 9-21-06	none		no camping

Area	River Mile	Expedition passed	Boat Connection	Interpretive Sign	Camping Rules
Washington City Access	68	5-25-04	ramp	yes*	contact City of Washington
Colter's Landing Access	Boeuf Cr. (78)	5-26-04	ramp	yes	river-approach-camping
New Haven City Access	81	5-26-04	ramp	yes*	contact City of New Haven
Hermann City Access	98	5-27-04	ramp	yes*	contact City of Hermann
Gasconade Park Access	105	5-27,28-04	ramp	yes	designated areas
Grand Bluff CA	inland (108)	5-29-04	none	yes	no camping
Tate Island CA	112	5-30-04	bank	yes	river-approach-camping
Chamois Access	118	5-30-04	ramp	yes*	contact City of Chamois
Mokane Access	125	6-1-04	ramp		designated areas
Smoky Waters CA	130-135	6-1,2-04	bank	yes	river-approach-camping
Bonnots Mill Access	Osage (130)	6-1-04	ramp		designated areas
Mari-Osa Access	Osage (130)	6-1-04	ramp		designated areas
Moreau 50 Access	Moreau (133)	6-3-04	ramp		no camping
Noren Access	144	6-4-04	ramp	yes	contact City of Jefferson
Capitol View Access	148	6-4-04	ramp		no camping
Marion Access	158	6-4-04	ramp	yes	designated areas
Hartsburg Access	160	6-5-04	ramp		no camping
Hart Creek CA	inland (160)	6-5-04	none		dispersed primitive camping
Marion Bottoms CA	158-163	6-5-04	bank		river-approach-camping plus designated areas
Plowboy Bend CA	167-172	6-5-04	bank		river-approach-camping plus designated areas
Providence Access	Perche Cr (170)	6-6-04	ramp		no camping
Eagle Bluffs CA	170-178	6-6-04	bank	yes	river-approach-camping plus designated areas
Rocheport Cave CA	inland (183)	6-7-04	bank		designated areas (Katy Trail access only)

Area	River Mile	Expedition passed		Boat Connection	Interpretive Sign	Camping Rules
Overton Bottoms (south) CA	178-185	6-7-04	9-19-06	bank		river-approach-camping
Taylor's Landing Access	185	6-7-04	9-19-06	ramp		designated areas
Diana Bend CA	187-190	6-7-04	9-19-06	bank		river-approach-camping plus designated areas
Davisdale CA	inland	6-7-04	9-19-06	bank		designated areas
Franklin Island CA	192-195	6-7-04	9-19-06	ramp	yes	designated areas
DeBourgmont Access	Lamine	6-8-04	9-18-06	ramp	yes	no camping
Glasgow Stump Island Access	226	6-10-04	9-18-06	ramp		contact City of Glasgow
Lewis Mill Access	L. Chariton	6-10-04	9-18-06	ramp		designated areas
Dalton Bottoms Access	Chariton (239)	6-12-04	9-18-06	bank		designated areas under construction
Brunswick Access	Grand (250)	6-13-04	9-18-06	ramp		designated areas
Miami Access	263	6-14-04	9-17-06	ramp	yes*	designated areas
Grand Pass CA	266-272	6-15-04	9-17-06	bank	yes	river-approach-camping plus designated areas
Baltimore Bend CA	inland (298)	6-19-04	9-16-06	none		dispersed primitive camping
Pigg's Landing Access	Fishing R. (334)	6-23-04	9-16-06	ramp		designated areas
Fort Osage Access	337	6-23-04	9-16-06	ramp	yes*	contact Jackson County Parks
Cooley Lake CA	341	6-24-04	9-15-06	ramp	yes (2)	river-approach-camping
Liberty Bend CA	351	6-25-04	9-15-06	bank		river-approach-camping
La Benite Access	353	6-25-04	9-15-06	ramp		contact City of Sugar Creek
Kansas City Riverfront Access	363	6-26-04	9-15-06	ramp		contact Kansas City
White Alloe Creek CA	inland (377)	6-30-04	9-15-06	ramp*		no camping
Parma Woods Range	inland (383)	6-30-04	9-15-06	none		no camping
Schimmel City Access	Platte (391)	7-1-04	9-15-06	ramp		no camping
Little Bean Marsh	inland (415)	7-3-04	9-14-06	none	yes	no camping
Bluffwoods CA & Annex	inland	7-5-04	9-14-06	none		designated areas

Area	River Mile	Expedition passed		Boat Connection	Interpretive Sign	Camping Rules
Jentell Brees Access	437	7-6-04	9-13-06	ramp	yes	river-approach-camping
Kneib Memorial CA	inland	7-6-04	9-13-06	none		no camping
Dupree Memorial CA	450	7-7-04	9-12-06	bank		river-approach-camping
French Bottoms Access	450	7-7-04	9-12-06	ramp	yes	contact City of St. Joseph
Sunbridge Hills CA	inland (458)	7-8-04	9-12-06	none	yes	no camping
Worthwine Island CA	457-460	7-8-04	9-11-06	bank		river-approach-camping plus designated areas
Nodaway Island Access	462.1	7-8-04	9-11-06	ramp	yes	river-approach-camping
Tom Brown Access	462.9	7-8-04	9-11-06	bank		river-approach-camping
Monkey Mountain CA	inland	7-8-04	9-11-06	none		designated areas
Payne Landing Access	477	7-9-04	9-11-06	ramp		river-approach-camping
Riverbreaks CA	inland (477)	7-9-04	9-11-06	none		designated areas
Bob Brown CA	483-487	7-10-04	9-11-06	none	yes	river-approach-camping plus designated areas
Rush Bottom CA	500-502	7-13-06	9-10-06	bank		river-approach-camping
Thurnau CA	508	7-13-06	9-10-06	ramp	yes	river-approach-camping plus designated areas
Deroin Bend CA	517-522	7-14-06	9-10-06	bank		river-approach-camping plus designated areas
Hoot Owl Bend Access	525	7-15-04	9-10-06	bank	yes	designated areas
Langdon Bend Access	531	7-15-04	9-10-06	ramp	yes	designated areas
Nishnabotna CA	542-544	7-16-04	9-10-06	bank		river-approach-camping
Watson Access	542	7-16-04	9-10-06	ramp	yes	designated areas
Star Hill School Prairie CA	inland	7-16,17-04	9-9-06	none	yes	designated areas
Lower Hamburg Bend CA	547-553	7-18-04	9-9-06	bank		river-approach-camping plus designated areas

Some Useful GPS Coordinates

Waypoint: St. Louis Arch
Latitude: 38.623877795
Longitude: -90.185475684

Waypoint: Frontier Park, St. Charles
Latitude: 38.780554006
Longitude: -90.480731241

Waypoint: St. Charles L & C Statue
Latitude: 38.776092151
Longitude: -90.482291448

Waypoint: First State Capitol,
St. Charles, Missouri
Latitude: 38.779922597
Longitude: -90.481990286

Waypoint: Discovery Expedition
Boat House, St. Charles, Missouri
Latitude: 38.773122024
Longitude: -90.482540977

Waypoint: Stone Hill Winery,
Hermann, Missouri
Latitude: 38.757139159
Longitude: -90.541934053

Waypoint: Hermann Riverfront
Latitude: 38.707867566
Longitude: -91.434631216

Waypoint: Jefferson City/Capitol
Latitude: 38.578492304
Longitude: -92.173694045

Waypoint: Native Stone Winery
Latitude: 38.662213938
Longitude: -92.338881660

Waypoint: Bull Rock Historic Site,
Jefferson City, Missouri
Latitude: 38.672780836
Longitude: -92.344028400

Waypoint: Central Dairy,
Jefferson City, Missouri
Latitude: 38.572393967
Longitude: -92.175631522

Waypoint: Les Bourgeois Bistro,
Rocheport, Missouri
Latitude: 38.968081487
Longitude: -92.550756223

Waypoint: Lexington Boat Ramp
Latitude: 39.195650577
Longitude: -93.884451379

Waypoint: Fort Osage
Latitude: 39.187403623
Longitude: -94.192833248

Waypoint: Discovery Center,
Kansas City Plaza, Missouri
Latitude: 39.040456958
Longitude: -94.574244040

Waypoint: Case Park (overlook with
Lewis & Clark statue), K.C., Missouri
Latitude: 39.104835004
Longitude: -94.592074695

Waypoint: English Park & Riverfront,
Parkville, Missouri
Latitude: 39.185158363
Longitude: -94.685170147

Waypoint: Harley Davidson Plant,
Platte County, Missouri
Latitude: 39.300569039
Longitude: -94.663682803

Waypoint: Jentell Breeze
Conservation Area boat ramp,
St. Joseph, Missouri
Latitude: 39.691022228
Longitude: -94.967197217

Waypoint: Wyeth Park overlook,
St. Joseph, Missouri
Latitude: 39.776884600
Longitude: -94.867372103

Waypoint: Sunset Grill restaurant,
boat ramp with fuel, St. Joseph, MO
Latitude: 39.801501496
Longitude: -94.877439690

Waypoint: French Bottom boat ramp
& casino, St. Joseph, Missouri
Latitude: 39.780767433
Longitude: -94.875714192

Waypoint: Weston State Park scenic
overlook, Weston, Missouri
Latitude: 39.387818951
Longitude: -94.880364136

Websites

For a complete listing of Lewis & Clark related events, visit
www.visitmo.com. For a complete listing of the Discovery
Expedition of St. Charles' reenactment schedule, visit
lewisandclark.net.

www.lewisandclark.state.mo.us
www.lewisandclarkstcharles.com • www.nps.gov/lecl
www.lewisandclarktrail.missouri.org
http://lewisclark.geog.missouri.edu
www.lewisandclarktrail.com • www.riverrelief.org
www.lewisandclarkexhibit.org • www.lewisandclark.org
www.moriver.org • www.lewisandclark200.org
www.friendsofbigmuddy.org • www.greatriverroad.com

Photo Credits

The majority of photographs for this book were taken by
the author. Many thanks to the following photographers
and agencies who contributed photographs for this
book: Terry Barner, Cape Girardeau Convention &
Visitors Bureau, Greater St. Charles Convention & Visitors
Bureau, Lewis & Clark State Historic Site in Hartford, Illinois,
the Missouri Folk Arts Council, Fred Lynch of the *Southeast
Missourian,* and the Missouri Division of Tourism. The
University of Nebraska Press, the American Philosophical
Society and the Bienecke Rare Books Collection at Yale Library
provided reprint permission for Clark's journal drawings.

Bibliography

Borwick, Jim, and Brett Dufur. *Forgotten Missourians Who Made History.* Rocheport: Pebble Publishing, 1996.

Clarke, Charles G. *The Men of the Lewis & Clark Expedition.* Lincoln: University of Nebraska Press, 2002.

Colter-Frick, L.R. *Courageous Colter and Companions.* Washington: Video Proof, 1997.

Corps of Engineers River Charts

Cutright, Paul Russell. *Lewis & Clark: Pioneering Naturalists.* Lincoln: University of Nebraska Press, 1989.

Denny, James. *Lewis and Clark Expedition Interpretative Sign Project.* Prepared for the Signs Workgroup of the Missouri Department of Natural Resources.

Denny, James. *Lewis and Clark in the Boonslick.* Boonville: Boonslick Historical Society, 2000.

Dictionary of Missouri Biography. Columbia: University of Missouri Press, 1999.

Dufur, Brett. *The Complete Katy Trail Guidebook.* Rocheport: Pebble Publishing, 2003.

Dufur, Brett. *Exploring Columbia & Central Missouri.* Rocheport: Pebble Publishing, 2003.

Ford McMillen, Margot. *A to Z Missouri: The Dictionary of Missouri Place Names.* Rocheport: Pebble Publishing, 1996.

Griffith, Cecil R. *The Missouri River: The River Rat's Guide to Missouri River History and Folklore.* N.p., 1974.

Lewis & Clark Bicentennial Lower Missouri River Guide to Recreation and Visitors Safety.

McKiernan, Mark F., and Roger D. Launius. *Missouri Folk Heroes of the 19th Century.* Independence: Independence Press, 1989.

Moulton, Gary. *The Definitive Journals of Lewis & Clark,* Vol. 8 of the Nebraska Edition. Lincoln: University of Nebraska Press, 1993.

Moulton, Gary. *The Journals of the Lewis & Clark Expedition,* Vol. 2, Lincoln: University of Nebraska Press, 1986.

Rogers, Ann. *Lewis & Clark in Missouri.* St. Louis: Meredco, 1993.

Index

Journal Entry Index by Date

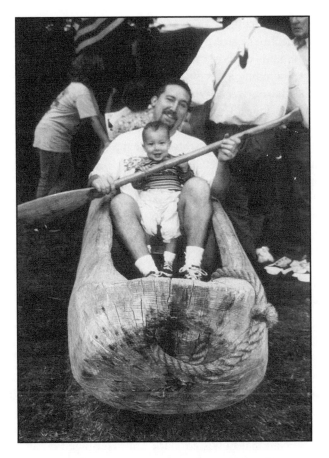

About the Author

Brett Dufur—shown above with his son, Everett—is also the leading author and contributor of *Lewis & Clark's Journey Across Missouri,* a full-color coffee-table compilation of the seven-part series on Lewis & Clark that he wrote for *Missouri Life Magazine.*

Brett is also the author of *The Complete Katy Trail Guidebook, The Katy Trail Nature Guide, Exploring Columbia & Central Missouri, Exploring Missouri Wine Country, Best of Missouri Hands* and *Show Me Mountain Biking.* He also co-authored *Forgotten Missourians Who Made History.*

Brett is the founder, editor and publisher at Pebble Publishing, Inc., a publisher of Missouri-related guidebooks.

Brett is also a member of the Discovery Expedition of St. Charles, an official reenactment group for the Lewis & Clark Bicentennial. Brett has logged hundreds of river miles on various Lewis & Clark reenactments, including a keelboat expedition from Wood River, Illinois, to St. Joseph, Missouri, in 1996 and a reenactment in replicas of Lewis & Clark's two pirogues, from Gavins Point Dam in South Dakota ending almost a thousand miles later in St. Charles, Missouri, in 1998.

Brett developed the first website for the Katy Trail in 1996, and the first website for the Lewis & Clark Trail in Missouri in 1998 in conjunction with the Missouri Association of Convention & Visitors Bureaus. He also developed websites for the Discovery Expedition of St. Charles, and for the Missouri River Communities Network.

His Lewis & Clark reenactment photographs have appeared in *Missouri Life Magazine,* the *St. Louis Post-Dispatch, Smithsonian Magazine, Midwest Traveler* magazine, the *Columbia Missourian,* on the cover of the Missouri Division of Tourism's *Missouri Vacation Planner,* on phone book covers and on book covers, including this book and the University of Missouri Press book *Lewis and Clark in Missouri.*

Brett has also worked with the Missouri Folk Arts Council on the Missouri River Traditions Project, interviewing and photographing individuals who live along the Missouri River in Missouri, Kansas and Nebraska, who have ties to the river through commerce, art or tradition. Brett is also a former board member of the Missouri River Communities Network and a founding member of the Mid-Missouri Manitou Bluffs Chapter of the National Lewis & Clark Trail Heritage Foundation. He also spearheaded the introduction of a river valley newspaper called the *Missouri River Valley Review,* in 1996, which published one glorious edition before he came to his senses. He graduated from the University of Missouri-Columbia School of Journalism in 1994.

Brett lives in Rocheport, Missouri, with his wife, Tawnee, and young son, Everett. He can be found most days getting tangled up in words, lollygagging on the trail, paddling the river, running his bookstore or renovating his old house. His most recent expedition involved camping in a tent on the living room floor with his son.

His bookstore is located at 205 Central Street in Rocheport, Missouri, a block from the Katy Trail. There you can browse 300-plus Missouri-related history and travel titles including an extensive Lewis & Clark section. Call Pebble Publishing at (573) 698-3903 or visit www.pebblepublishing.com.

Brett is available to give slide shows about the Lewis & Clark Trail in Missouri and his river travels.